lucky coat anywhere

Also by Michael Burkard

Poetry:

In a White Light, 1978
None, River, 1979
Some Time in the Winter (chapbook), 1979
Ruby for Grief, 1981
The Fires They Kept, 1986
Fictions from the Self, 1988
My Secret Boat (A Notebook of Prose and Poems), 1990
My Brother Makes a Toast but Uses by Mistake His Name (chapbook), 1992
Three (chapbook), 1997
Entire Dilemma, 1998
Pennslvania Collection Agency, 2001
Unsleeping, 2001
Envelope of Night: Selected and Uncollected Poems, 1966-1990, 2008

Drawings:
(Available through Blurb.com)

Michael Burkard, 2010
a flower with milk in a shadow beside it, 2010
one day my face, 2010

Recordings:

who do voodoo (improvised songs), 2009

lucky coat anywhere

poems by

Michael Burkard

NIGHTBOAT BOOKS

CALLICOON, NEW YORK

Contents

for Marion and Abe

Sólo sabiamos que una recta, si quiere, puede ser curva o quebrada
y que las estrellas errantes son niños que ignoran la aritmética.

We knew only that a straight line, if it likes, can be curved or broken
and that wandering stars are children who don't know arithmetic.

Los Angeles Colegiales
(The Grade School Angels)

Rafael Alberti
(translated by Mark Strand)

I

Black Horses in White Envelopes

—for mpt

1
Boxes of meaning.

2
Little books about fire.

3
Kim's drawing:
"Mask" in bed — "I don't want
dad to know I'm afraid of
anything."

4
Umbrella angel.
Suit of death.
When relatives
want to disappear.

5
The word "erotica"
outweighed all the other clouds.

6
When talking about black horses
in white envelopes we are obviously
talking about very small horses.
It is important to tell just how,

if at all, the horses died, and to
be precise as to whether the horses
are figuratively dead or really dead.
The envelopes become less and less
important.

7

But days later the envelopes
become more important in unexpected
ways. You realize very deeply
they are white, not off-white
or almost-white or anything-else-
white but white. They are also
very small, not much larger
than the small black horses.

8

Unspeakable boxes of the small
riders on the small black horses
placed in small white envelopes.
These boxes however small remain
good for breathing, fine for
breathing, but most of all remind
riders and horses and envelopes
alike of what a small gift breathing
is.

9

Fire *is* the next time.
A little fire to read a little
book by by a little rider resting
her little horse before she remounts
to enter little envelope.

10

Father, dad, do you see how small
your daughter has become, if even
small for just a moment? As children
we often have this strange but adhesive
and natural sensation of the small.
It colors a world.

11

To color a world: black and white are colors.
We realize this now from the lack of black
and white films and black and white photography.
Together they served as one of the Masks Kim
could wear, Donna could wear, I could wear.

12

At the Hotel Vallejo you could rent
an umbrella for two dollars an afternoon,
death for five dollars an evening,
a relative for ten dollars (breakfast included),
and a suit of death for fifteen
(a special weekend rate).
If you rented the whole package you
could also disappear for a week
for another five dollars. It is of no
use to fall away from the hotel or to
pretend you are not interested.
Face it, M., you are interested.
Tell Donna.

14

Outside the hotel are small riders
on small horses and a word you cannot find.
The horses have not died.
The clouds have not died.
No one has died or come to.

The Found Face Girl

A boy who heard he could care for The Found Face Girl.

dragging dead people into 12-step meetings

in my last dream i had rapid oral sex with someone i paid $100 to
before we entered the meeting

and then someone had to call out because a land deal was being
claimed

Lunar Floor Lipstick
the killers and the libraries and the lifelong friends

"everything in isolation from everything else"

I have a Charlie Horse on the brain
I have snow on the forehead
Fuentes is arriving Thursday and my mother isn't ready —
she is supposedly "dead" to this world —
I don't know.

"each flower is its own individual facing its own way" —
then my mother is still facing F. and me and the orchids she planted too

i have taken a vow of poetry
The Found Face Girl said

She says she does not know from the film on van Gogh at Arles
whether the Portrait of Bach is something he painted or whether
he painted it as part of the room painting, on the wall as one of
his "things" — a portrait by another? She will find out —

I tell The Found Face Girl that in the city I grew up in, in the "town"
I grew up in, that i had called it "the town that took the downtown down,"
and that the aqueduct van Gogh painted — which still has trains running
over(?)/under(?) it near his yellow house — that this compares favorably
with my town's "Living Bridge," a structure which went nowhere, which
"lived" for about thirty years and then the same people who made money
taking the downtown down helped decide to reopen the closed off
        downtown
and also to take down the living bridge. A short snowy history.

de Kooning says "the sun has four windows"
(n/ s/ e/ w)

the living bridge had ten windows — it didn't help / van Gogh's
        aqueduct needs
none / The Found Face Girl has an extra window

van Gogh is quarterbacking the old Los Angeles Rams
on weekdays he is painting the letters of the Hollywood Land sign

people jump from or collapse their lives from — i want to read a memoir
of one who came close to his or her appointed letter and stopped
and went back to life as we know it

de Kooning describes himself as "a slipping glimpser"
a glimpser who falls

a fork who falls
a matchbook who falls
a sunflower who falls

who falls with the sunflower?
who falls with the coffee?
a simplicity who falls?
a guitar who falls?

who falls with Fuentes and Lisa's batch of money?
the windows of the living bridge were numerous but were placed in
    a position
of smallness so that the eventual collapse of the bridge could be said
    to guarantee
that it would be these small positional windows which would fall first

a mayor who falls
a man who reads a regular deck of cards for people and he falls
a few readers who fall because of his readings before he does

sometimes in his own yellow house
Carlos senses that one of the readees could still be falling

if isolation has an f
it could happen — you could isolate to an almost exhibitionist extent

you could have trouble with words
like you have trouble with kites

but you could keep falling
and it would have more to do with the cards than the words

when on of my mother's wives threatened to kill herself —
well announced the threat as a thought more than actually threatened —
e.g. I was going to throw myself under the train
    I was going to shoot myself

when these were "announced" it was obviously not a time
when things were good and well and my mother would say —

but these were positional fallings too
a reach for the harbor from far inland

who could be blamed for falling?
one of my mother's wives' husbands
(and there were many of both)

went into the cellar as if he was a "both" —
he structured a secret world around the objects there —
which included socks — and he began passing the socks
through the air while one of the wives' was upstairs shooting
a gun off — he was a quarterback but there was no end to this

a window became a sacrament
the hamper became another person

he would never read cards again (not true)
he would never again walk past his own cough

his uncle said I will fall into your card game if you let me
        I will fall with your organized fantasies if only you let me in

The Found Face Girl
said that when she had read Hughes' *Shakespeare in Harlem*
she had taken the title literally, that she wanted
Shakespeare's figure to be there,
and it was through that door she understood the poem
"Went home" to Shakespeare just as much as "to her ma."

She identifies with the hinge of Hughes'
"So" which begins the fourth and final stanza.
She sees "Hughes" ticket, joker, Buick.
No man will drive my little Buick she says, taking from,
paraphrasing Hughes.

I am not saved. Carlos is recalling the face of a readee,
the reader of the cards, he is not thinking Hughes'
What makes a woman / Treat a man so bad

he is phrasing What makes a man / Treat a man so bad.
I am not saved. You had a home, but not for that night.

I threw you out into the unsaving cold.
I made fun of you.
I told your mother no soap.
Your dog "Queenie" was due with her pups
and even the animal kingdom could not arouse my sympathies.
I threw you out in order to have another voice.
One was river enough but not for me you know.
I told you the cards knew just where you were headed.
I could see from the stilted position of your head you thought so too.

You told me more roads with your head than I could have ever thought up.
You'd think this would have softened me but no.
Deeper, much deeper, I thought I was at the end.
The Coast of Holland. Or France.
Spain with a moan and a murmur and a pear.
Your shirtsleeves began to behave like eyes.
I wake up away and I don't know how to make up for this.
I can't say so.
Jason says that when you walk down the street in Provincetown
"You have to reinvent yourself every time."
He loves this possibility, this owning.
I was something as dull as an eight of clubs
a weightless death spotted in someone else's worlds — Aleixandre's? —
a sea spotted like a hand waving rapidly between / among a few sea-trees.
A genuine sense of the Found Face Girl long before she appeared
or could ever be thought to appear.

The Found Face Girl's tenderness with both Carlos and my mother.
The same tenderness. This wasn't easy to accomplish or to do.
She was / is genuine like you.
I am afraid
I will run out of you and be all by myself and then run out of myself too.
I remember when you were trying to write in this small space in one of
    your closets.
I was on one small hill looking down to a hill which was also small
which led to your place.
I could not spell anything with a k in it.
I could not spell the world, the recorded world.
Neither could you.
Or so it seemed Or so you said sometimes.

Ghost Reader (A Street in Brooklyn)

you had to learn something from lists
of advice: the heart without said heart knowing:
the beer and the job and the boss without being sensible:
river of heart does not flow even after a few with the boss:
give it up: you are not his / he is not yours:
house but by:
buy moon mine:

there's a self destructive memory of another life
just after the rain falling: there's your trial by error
and that Lydia like greeting: Jean has a resulting energy:
i am not for or against a night in Venice
i am not for or against the wandering horses

something coming largely undone:
Hikmet's "I still have pictures of me taken there…"
i am still taken
still photographs by unstill waters —
still there is an idol "ended up" as i reacted to red book
white book —what would it be like to be an animal
without a name Paul said— the word dreamer—
it would be a word dreamer without a word and if you
leaned your head slowly just so someone there would
talk to you—now if i had sent bob's reddish horses
we could have used them for the cover—always this
sense of using—it is like an infection—this is

how you can get me home again— tell me you have run out
on the key—tell me the flute and the viola and the complicate
are lined up like the furniture we saw with our eyes—same
hill beyond shadow, same life as life was with you—

I still have pictures of me taken there—
was interrupted hours ago by another knock on the door
and another child—a brother later met on the corner
took my hand—I took his—

*

it is just something to say
it is a way of not finally trusting in any words or places
like them—Bourgeois' *Light Bulb Attempt at Self-Knowledge*, 1948
is a wonderful clasp and joke on myself—
it too is a k
as far as i am concerned—it is like my extravagant home sometimes
filled with rain and kisses and other k—
and here it comes w and l b
(l and b) to play—LB's initials in the light bulb—
the strange promises z made to m and to h are further discussed—
chekhov is invited to see b
sharon is asked to ask t something
ver y palpar
we love to create light and birds and pansies and grades to
enumerate schools by and names to name teachers by and unknown names
to name windows by—
and d will assume chris' name as i did
and q will assume the identity of some strange punctuation mark
and I will assume a prone position in the meeting of the addicts
because i feel guilty about hopkins—these kinds of dreams are
tree limbs—a voice not unlike sharon's blesses me from an indigo
or a kind of indigo map of a map's world—the dream sense has
briefly doubled upon itself—no doors are slammed—
the deathlife has taken another job and requests a meeting with c
—the alphabet is tired
—i remember one wing of the alphabet kept in the school of missing
things: words, children, windows: none were more sought after yet
more homeless: one's classic insomnia took a seat next to a beloved
windmill, one's sky became another girl's autumn, one's feeling became
another boy's a, or worldless game. One chance became one mirror,
the girl's painting of the horse became the forest the horse had come

from. One thing requested respected as a word. One talker said I am just as lost. And capitalizing myself does not help. A helper became a cup of coffee. The number 19 the moon. My little son sat with Louise and sat closer when he said my father wanted me to be a girl. I am hoping for a tiny newborn. He said he would glance.

*

the murder starts
i am in another country—
my sister calls me to tell me the murder has started—
we momentarily confuse each other because i think she means
the murder has started in another country
but she is simply reiterating the fact i am in another country
but because i am another country— actually am at an inn too—
because i am inn another country
i am in
i am
inn—
the murder starts with the man having asked for money on the subway
stairway ledge as he is prone and perhaps really perhaps asleep
—his sleep is even like this word perhaps here
slightly out of place
the kind someone would say don't use don't use that radar
—but he used it
—so many passersby but once in awhile of course someone puts
money in his cap which is part of his hand
—the murder starts because someone hates him
even this space he uses is hated
it is meant as everything by some hater
an in the word lux for light
or las sambras for the shadows
or the one door of the word lifted onto one door
Y recuerdo
maybe all he was reported as saying
Y recuerdo
nada más nada más
nada más—

it is in the one rooster i was robbed of my rob and struck
not only by conversation but by this strange hammer
and the blow of it
and the collapse of it
the and of it
—camisero

*

let's see if you leave a lot out people will not guess Ashbery's
"clean washed sea" —
instead will think of midwinter some other gyration from themselves
for their own missing lives lives which were like any lives
talking
how do you say
inconsistently—i place a yellow t shirt upon the already floor
for the already cat panther and sheerly the cat makes an inconsistent
move to the front door which is down an andre dubus like stairway
an andre like photograph
a hundred or even thousands of eric berlin signs
or a hundred or even thousand eric berlin radios
or matt garite banisters or clocks he has presumed in the eventual
tenderness of his own heart—like a ghost reader
or a ghost reader who has returned in your night to tell you how
to turn the energy of a dream into a space that can actually help
you inhabit your own heart the next day—so you don't armor yourself
too heavily or armour yourself too heavily either—
it's sort of the same thing when you lean into it—
better than the shirt can but that isn't as supposedly/ always as true
as one seems—the shirt is one—when you were homeless
you held on to your clothes in a like manner—
hey people did not like you
that was obvious
your clothing was a different thing
any clothing you could find
you became a version of a scarce crow you saw in an art museum
on a cold day before they asked you to leave ("they")—
your thinking was hey i am more like this framed space suit stuffed
with used clothing than anything else in here or even the thing
itself—talk to me for god's sake—okay i feel homeless in a

different sense now
when i do these books such as unsleeping—it's like a part of
myself has betrayed part of myself—when you were on the street
well what is it like now
i mean do you ever feel equally or almost equally betrayed?

*

don't know what imaginable or unimaginable circumstances
played upon her—
needless in the night
i saw my work working on my father and my friend who were
talking
how do you say
inconsistently—and when one smaller reader left before
anyone in the audience could say hey stop i want to talk with you
about how you talked to us—but this sounds very hostile doesn't it
very much a milieu or a therapist
someone said i wanted help who meant to say i needed help
but the help was an expensive one hundred and sixty dollars an hour
and hour
as i type that out in print i see how long the amount takes to say
i saw my father working on the home small accounts standing he did
at his dresser
i saw my father close the door to heaven when he went with my mother
to talk with her
i saw an endless parrot or so i thought
this endless parrot was the first bird of spring one year
because i walked early down a new york street
a brooklyn street when i looked in the window and saw
then i realized this is spring the first day for our species
and therefore and therefore
not about to answer your call because of all the implicit criticism
in tone and yes i do not say some words right and yes i am the one
who has let himself be betrayed much by himself in matters of self
importance and also art is it my art i don't know it is what i do
how do you say small when the radio no longer uses that word
nothing is ever small anymore in this small literal box of a radio
or hand held small world too

what happened to my friend who was run down by a bicycle only
a few weeks after being set up mugged two people followed in a car
while one followed on the street
then it was as if a sudden photograph entered his room
if we sleep in the same room together even though you seem a
canyon away are you wanting to sleep with me in the endless
endless night?

Ghost Text

Ghost Text:

For a long time
I was the only
child in my
neighborhood.

can't comb hair
at night

turning
a shoe over

"a piece of paper
and a book
up at the house"

"talk about the part of
me who disappears"

Okay, Okay

Okay, okay. I am driving out to find you. I am going to kiss you
again. About to kiss you. Kiss you for an hour before we are
found or turn ourselves in. the sound of an "s" and the sound
of a "t." Kissing drives right down the avenue and straight into
the dream. No sleep necessary. But I wake up with the
window propped on my knees, reading the window like a night
book. Then I remember our discussion of kissing. The woman
in the Klee Museum. the clerk who made too much change.
The man who asked where he could find other ghosts...

The Woman in the Klee Museum

"C" died. Someone in the alphabet is always dying. Each letter climbs down into the grave like a lost cloud before a moon cycle or a door cycle completes. Yes, "K" hung out too long. Yes, "N" was too lazy (simply eating the marijuana without even heating it). Yes, "M" exclaimed "Placebo!"— was never heard. No. "C's" parent never followed. My shirt convinced me very very quietly she was following on a local road, she would turn up in the darkness of the reading, she would understand my wish and my choice. But the road made it easy and I found my way to the museum's rooftop, and I peered through the skylight until I could read who owned which painting. One had been painted onto burlap, one had been compared to unhappiness. But I could hardly read the writing.

Five

Chris writes *White Hour* as a complete book. He includes
clocks, for me and me alone he also includes a bag. My small
panther peers into the same empty valise which received
genuine compliments the other night when it was not empty.
Chris has not included enough light, so we agree to meet
downtown—after a fact, after a lamp. The table in the wee
corner with the flask of the gone moon daring us. We had four,
no, five drinks. Then we went sideways. Then we talked about
five. We drew 5 as often as we could. We exchanged math
stories and someone—not a fan of moonlight— overheard us
and looked at us like we were terrible. We asked someone else
to dance. I make five out to be black-and-white. What do you
make it out to be? At five in the morning, unable to sleep, I try
writing in an old notebook. The card of the inn is there. It is
gentle with shadows and it is the day. I can't make out the
signature on the back of the card. I don't' know which what tape
I mailed "them" which "they" say "they" received. The last four
words of the card read "… when you are here." The fifth word
from the end looks like "when" too. The second when— if it is
when—I am not sure—the second when almost looks like well.
Five edges of the moon look back at me through the window
because I have stared much too long at the one low moon. And
I haven't worn my reading glasses to make out "when." I never
wear the glasses enough. Interesting mistakes are made. Unlike
here, the mistakes are usually more interesting than what was there.

Welcome to Kensington Road

Dear Herr T. Tranströmer,

It's pretty tough when you are asked to join a house at the last minute. Such a fate befell me on Tuesday, which happened also to be All Hollow's Eve. Whatever that means.

I find lists which I can't comprehend: "Blue Rangers," "god acting anonymously," "the invasion of spelling," "Draw B's man who talks too fast—like me and John" (with this last one I know at least what the first half means, but I haven't ever seen the man—I know also who I mean by John—but how the two of us, why the two of us…).

I like houses where when you come in the front door there is nothing but space for awhile. There are a few candles on a nearby/final table. And this next part is easy: a friend or two, a James and/or a Lisa, greeting you—it is to be their house, this is the rumor. Mary is across the street. Linda is on a nearby corner. So many gentlemen are exchanging papers that none of us friends notices the bicycle.

There is no part for me in this house. I am an envelope, and late at that. No, just an envelope.

That's enough.

It seems easy.

I will buy a dog for them. I will recover completely. I too will understand "Welcome to Kensington Road," and I will partake of this understanding.

Yet there is always an insidious invective underneath a love-list, a delivery, a kindness. Spokes spoken. Double facts. High windows and last sun too across streets.

Still,

don't you think math is too easy? Too blank (my mother is blank, my book is blank, my blank is very blank).

My verbs are weak (don't tell my heart).

I hate the son of my insurance man.

The heavy load of the eye aims its futile crossbow at the boy who has called from a new poem. What a booth, what a cell to not tell everything to your own heart from.

Tell someone: the photographer left his story on Clive Street.

Or was it *Olive* Street?

This is will count.

Like the no in my bottom crown.

Like the nurse who shops at lunch.

You have made her female, not me.

I was the one who tried saying hello to her.

I had a photograph of my childhood (with a d) underneath my arm.

A childhood would be ridiculous without a d.

One if by Land

I can't see myself
—I've eaten two car stories.
I asked a friend to pose at the base of a skyscraper
—but he said he didn't want to become a souvenir.

There is no more alone time in the world
or time out.
No more corners.
A tree breaches a fact in a sister's sleep

but no one else is troubled.
If I could just observe for awhile—
so much to promise—
so much to clear up.

Yesterday the cars I saw looked like tribal
lines—a funeral was slowing ebbing around
a corner. I could see flowers in the wrong sky.
The sky was wrong because it belonged to the sky.

Dog's Ear

Has made, has not, has too—then the light overhead doesn't really flicker or dim—but it reminds the room of February—a snowmound upside down on a stranger's ceiling. Just when it seems almost plausible to get away with getting to the film late, or offering sex to someone from my past who remains in the past (a sexual fantasy in which one returns to a street and actually stays there—the sex stays there too, in the house-where-the-writerly-couple is away at least a third of the weekends of the year—a young girl watches an old clip of *Invaders from Mars*—two letters in the alphabet stand for one—she wants to rent the old thing now—the barbed wire marks on the back of the bad-guy and bad-girl necks in the film—even the mother and father become bad-girl/guy—the father actually cycles through an entire lifetime of personality change after a post breakfast walk to examine the dune, to examine the dream—in the film the boy's dream is the dream of a boy's life—because it brings him round straight to a truer mother—Tessa says she based one of her composition notebook/texts/landscapes—What *are* these things anyway?—upon a letter sinking in the sand, and then another letter, until letters of the alphabet like people were reduced to true difficulties—there just wasn't as much to go around as you would think or as it ap-peared—the end appeared and Tessa said she wanted to watch the film one more time sometime next week, but then from a hill)—and in the past the hill climbed near a farmer's yard, and when you leaned into your mother or father's neck or the haphazard neck of a cop on the chance you lived in a very strange town where you could and would want to lean there—well from that hill I see an animal too, maybe a progression, and unnecessary wilderness.

What Do You See?

I see a punch coming toward me.
I see my father has not heard from my brother who for some
    reason is in California, where he rarely is, and even rarer is
    my father's lucky intuition my brother has been abducted.
I see a dream where the shadows of the snow reveal the old part
    of the cemetery to the wandering couple instead of revealing
    the new stones area, and since the couple is each alive, one
    unto one and one unto another, I see them as hunting for
    "new stones."

Not meant to be a typical dream or zone. I am talking more
    for myself, using dream the way you might use a street or a
    landscape or a small yard where you could rest. A small
    where sumac could make me.

I see Boston, I see France, I see Asta's underpants.
I see a man living in Mexico half the time and living in a flame-lie
    the rest of the year.
See the even confined brown dollar. Bigger money is better.
Michael, Linda, little wire.

Not meant to name no one or anyone or no one else.

*Be*linda
Be quick.
Don Quix-it.

I will never see you again.

Inside the Spaceship
Near the End of the Movie

It isn't true. We've had a few mean words—mean like the light
of the doll. Drew the "boat, town" (baten—byn)—then in a
meaner-than-a-childhood Bill spoke up from the back: "And
why isn't that done?"

About six miles from the night lamp you can find the boat
and the rope and the string and the gloves and the shovel they
used to

1)   not identify themselves to "Chuck" or any patriot with a
name like that ("Chip," "Sonny")—all except one face dressed in
a blue shirt. That house's heat where they started from was
blowing too hard for so early in the winter and you can see if you
look a little closely that the shirt is actually billowing just a bit.
The face is billowing slightly too. This is because of eating and
fluids and not the heat. The blue color billows like someone
telling him don't do this right now. It will ruin a friendship. You
are going to wake up in the middle of the so-called-night and
realize you are waking up in the middle of the so-called-night.

2)   Stop abruptly leaving the Sunday meal. No one under-
stands the alternatives better or more shapely than you.

Chris and I Attend the Same Movie
Thinking of the Same Man and the Same Woman

But we don't' tell anyone and we don't tell each other.
The movie rocks with childhood and war.
Across the smallish city I have discarded even the *Heartbreak*
Hotel EP my Uncle Rudolph and Aunt Alice had bought for
me. Or had given me $1.29 to buy. Or it's the photograph of
Presley wearing a raincoat, a profile, and it's black-and-white
and even grey after you see the yellow lettering. And Across-town
in still another smallish city the landlord is running out of the
garage with his hands held over his eighty-year-old ears.
Chris and I buy a notebook calendar together at the intermission,
instead of candy. We talk about it. We drown in the indecision.
On page forty-five-or-six Presley is facing the camera with some
brick in back of him. There's a woman wearing a kerchief to his
actual right. There's a partial face behind a partial newspaper
over his left raincoated shoulder. He's even wearing a thinnish
tie. He looks like a black and white version of some other actor
now or since then. Or he looks like a brother or a cousin
someone up or down the street has. Has but later.
It's the same photo session. It's too late.

It's Not Too Late

Someday I want to know the woman in the kerchief. Someday I want to know the object and the source or the other shadow up front. Someday I want to give my halfway hellish greeting cards to miracle workers. I am asking you for change he says. Maybe I should put a blue towel in this.

Some ideas occurred to me. I am just trying to write some things down. Like Chris' knee touched my knee. Like: hey, Jimmy's hand came out of nowhere for said Mason Dots™.

One evening at the Exeter in Boston in a thick throng I asked for Mason Dots™ right after someone waiting impatiently for his popcorn said "Mason Dots™. NO ONE eats those things anymore."

And there I was. Still in his shot ear. Buffoon for an evening. sitting down too to watch the movie (Antonioni?).

But Let's Get Back to
Chris and Chris' Mother

Don't drink too much coffee, but there's another photograph I
am interested in. Eva Hesse is standing with her father at an
opening at the Graham Gallery in New York City. There is no
way I am not going shopping before this rare winter day of sun
stops. Driving to drive and driving to drive slowly.

The opening of "Abstract Inflationism and Stuffed
Expressionism."

It's getting hot and it's getting darker.

New York. March 1966.

I may not be much but I am all I think about (quote/unquote).

March 1966. My life is collapsing very fast. It's a mess.

Frank O'Hara: one last time I love you.

We love you (quote/unquote).

John Yau writes/talks: "solitariness is the one thing we have
in common."

Yau *on* O'Hara. Provincetown. FAWC. The year 2000.

Meditation Brought about by George Bogin's Translation of Jules Supervielle's Poem "The Sea"

Something in the letter found in the box, and something just out there in the winter white, and something in the sky, something less than discontent: sheer light blue through one window, at least for now — something in the way you got out of her, I mean got out of the relationship, something in the way you got out of the relationship truly neglected the vision of the nova you then brought to George (the nova in the sky, not the car. And not the "no cars in the sky" which the kindergarten teacher actually warned her class about before the little ones began drawing. Not the nova car I wrecked and was lucky to have not placed in the sky along with myself. Appropriate white man constellation: el nova in el sky). And something in my endless awkwardness when George would tell me I had more feeling than any of the others, I was ashes with feeling… and my awkwardness with this was not unlike the awkward and incomplete version I or I-and-Lisa brought to George about the sky nova flash, incredible distance/ closeness / vastness / vanishing witnessed by us the night before

—something in the torn pieces of blue paper the little girl has typed upon, a letter to her friend she calls it, but also angry at the friend she says for not wearing a dress the two of them as later the letter tries to explain had planned… ashes with feeling…

Something, something, but you can't put your finger on it. The old postcard? The postcard which you referred to as "pre-car." The postcard you felt this dis-ease looking at but kept anyway in an isolated place where you were bound to see it again, by itself, and yet not quite see anything or anything you could be sure of because of this dis-ease. Ashes with feeling? Another version of it? As a writer with more feeling

than the others, isn't there a pressure upon you to know what you are
talking about, or at least to not know in some manner which would reveal
itself as acceptance, not pretended but felt? Is this the feeling, to
be a few moments from it, and still feel it?

What about George's feelings? Doesn't it take a feeler to recognize
another feeler? What about Lisa's feelings? What about another George,
who walked into the recovery meeting like he was a friend of Al Capone's,
appropriately oblivious. Maybe there's a planet named Capone? Lisa?

Remember Bob looking at a card you also had, and unlike this village-
corner-card of dis-ease this other card is a corner you like, ashes
with feeling again, but Bob looks at the card for just a moment and
sees a person/figure walking on the street and you had never for these
years and all this looking seen this figure. The figure is all but gone,
erased, erased ashes, but Bob sees it, Bob with his magic eye… a retina
with more feeling than the others… an iris with more feeling than the
others… Is that it? Is that him? Who is he?

George Bogin translated many poems by Jules Supervielle. Today I am
looking at a copy of wonderful old IRONWOOD #23, Michael
      Cuddihy's magazine,
incredible Michael Cuddihy with incredible retina and iris and ashes.
I am saying to myself let's look at some of the poems in this issue because
since I had a few in there myself I probably never really took a close look
at anyone else's — and some of this feels true — or it could be my bad
memory for poems which has never improved despite anyone's feelings or
retina— or it is a sideways memory which remembers a life just to the
side of everyone's poems, not unlike (again) ashes, or the retina dashing
off to another place it accounts for, sometimes truly, sometimes counter-
fit. I started to read a poem by Carruth, I read a part of it, a favorite
reading habit of mine, just parts, especially with favorite poets…
you wouldn't think this was true, but it is, if I am reading you line

by line all the time I am probably feeling trapped, and with more feeling
than the others this is a major turn-off, not unlike turning off not only
the road but the wrong road at the wrong time...

I start to read a poem by Carruth, I read part of it, and then I see
George's translations are in there, and I look at two and feel this
slight turning going on. Something in me knows this feeling.
—But is there a wrong time? Is there a wrong road? Is there a wrong
sea? A wrong sea...

In a few moments or a minute or two I am moving small boxes, cigar boxes.
The house I am living in is being town up upstairs, and I am moving small
boxes, still another box. And knowing it is letters I decide to look inside
and pretty quickly among about one hundred or more pieces of paper I come
across accidentally a letter from Ruth Bogin written just after George's
death. And now I am wanting to drive somewhere, this feeling of slight
turning is turning into trapped, and I don't care if it's a wrong road
or a wrong road to a wrong sea at anytime: I want to come up with an excuse
to get moving, to get away from something, with me more feeling than the
others, me with more ashes in my retina than the others. Me with endless
vacations at wrong seas.

But a part of me like a part of someone's poem is saying just stay still
and sit with these poems/translations of George's and Jules' — and there
is one translation entitled "The Sea" and I don't read the whole ting
but the first half or so is very unlike any poem or drawing about the sea
I have ever heard — the poem is on to something, and as I say that now I
also have this sense that the poem "about" the sea has also put me on to
myself, and George, and a recollection of many things, and people I have
not met, and people I would deeply like to see again, people when I got
to know George a little bit, and Lisa, and whatever that was in the sky.

And I have some vague memory of a telephone call to George when I received from him a book of his own poems, making the call from the Waters' house, from the warm climate, and I have this continual sense that his book-title included the word "wave." The sense is now a word which is a continuum, a wave. And George's face merges with Arthur's, as it has before, and I see George's wife, Ruth, and his daughter, Nina, neither of whom I have ever seen.

a retreat of chairs

some of my favorite handwriting isn't there
—that should be no surprise.
you want to be a shore to a wounded boy…

in one sketchbook some pages are kept there
to keep them safe and flat—how can i talk about this?—

and on/within one early page is a piece of writing
and a piece of drawing—the drawing is very heavy ink—

gone over and over and over—and seemed
for the longest time what made the pages worth keeping

the writing went (in one light pen at the very top)
4/30

(and i think it was 1970—i was working in a hospital)

4/30
The Train Lying Low

She sd she didn't recognize me
and that brought me down to
trains lying low.

there's a quick dark mark through the writing—and another
quick line through the "to" and near the heavy ink—

you want to hold a current in your heart as if it's a place —
you want to call someone, what's wrong with that?

what's wrong...

retreat of chairs (2)

the rest of the page reads
    4/31 crossed out (although now the idea of a world with a
    4/31 appeals to me)

4/31 is crossed out for 5/1

Long live poetry without friends
This horizontal force, a boxcar
speeding midst everything (i want my midst handwriting to read
unlit but it doesn't, it won't)
        —horizontal, girls
in red stockings sliding on the seats of
the subway to make space for an old
worn somebody in a captain's clothes—
has he considered the color, the pitch
the hemorrhage of a star collapsing
into its self-aura of lives, forces, planes,
a geometric blackness that blazes, his imagination
                (i want my handwriting
                to read his unequation)
old wood, an eater late at night when (where?) no one
can watch what his mouth swallows—
              (before i begin copying this
i thought eater read <u>earth</u>—but it doesn't—
it stops at "swallows"—the ink is the same as the ink
of the heavier lines in the geometric drawing—it is all
one stanza and the drawing moves heavily next to <u>friends</u> and <u>boxcar</u>
and there is an outside chance it inks out some word next to
<u>girls</u>

retreat of chairs (3)

at one university you can request, on your birthday,
and you have to provide proof it is your birthday
beyond the records the university currently keeps,
and you may be called upon to do this in front of
a strange panel, and then you will exchange places
with one member of the panel, for a few minutes, to
see what you yourself would have thought of this
additional birthday "evidence," whether you would have
considered it evidence of any kind, whether you would
have wanted to shout the candidate down, even if the
candidate reminds you of yourself, as is so possible,
or reminds you of a brief birthday moment, somewhere
"back" in time, almost as if time did have a back
to it, or a backside, which in a sense it may have
(once, looking at a possible drawing possibly explaining
what you would see if you could see all the way to the
"end" of the universe, the drawing revealed the back of
your head, or the head of one like you, as if time did
indeed have a backside—your own!)—but in any case
this evidentiary hearing will not last long, nor will
the exchange of roles, and you are glad for that, you
are glad for a token chance to be on the other side of
a desk, you are glad for a moment desks are still used,
you think of a desk where a birthday gift or dress or
slacks was laid out, by someone who supposedly only came
to your house on birthdays or anniversaries, someone who
lived somewhere in the town, or in the city a few miles
from you, someone who was said to live where anyone would
live

retreat of chairs (4)

at this one university you can request to go on
a retreat of chairs. you have to be a chair. you
cannot be the chair of a suicide. nor can there be
a suicide's chair within three generations of your
family or any of your last family. this evidence too
is not simply a drop in the bucket, and it is not
gathered that simply either. but if you are a chair
you may go on this retreat, and you get to be with
other chairs, anonymous chairs, chairs of blue, hard
chairs, chairs you thought you knew but you never knew,
the chair of the sea (or so the chair will say), the
infamous "other" chair, the chair you heard so much
about, the vulnerable chair, there is always one of
those chairs in every crowd, but usually you are the
last to know it, there is also the secret chair (as
there is also a secret door and a secret window, but
much more of that later)—there is the chair of chairs—
or did we mention that chair—there is the chair
which is longing to be a chair, there is a chair which
would like to be a suicide but will not say so under
any circumstance or chair, there is usually an interim
chair somewhere around—the interim chair is a very
uncomfortable chair—it is a hard chair to be in—
then there is the chair of the gallows
        the chair of the hands
the chair of the sun and the chair of the easy moon
and the chair of the shoulders bent to the ground—
these latter chairs are never there or never invited—
or they are simply "overlooked"—no one is sure which

—of course if you understood the rain
you would understand the chairs

—place the lamps as close to your head
as possible

—you read a man his rights once
—but then a voice over your voice

—have you ever read a woman her rights?
her rites? was the voice which read over your voice

a woman's voice or a man's voice or your wife's voice
and in any case could you distinguish the voice from

any of these conditions
or identities or even your own voice?

as a chair, if you were to become a chair,
do you have a voice?

does a pigeon have a right to cross the street
or are you about the run the pigeon down?

last rites: is the chair a rite? is a puzzle
leaving for death or some other place in-between?

—of course if you are planning to take a chair with you
there is not much of a need to identify any voice,

any condition, any moment or puzzle or piece

—i am not a c or a chair
—i am not a member of the "Glowworm" group at school

—i am not a c or a chair
—i am not a member of a moment she never crossed

—in this life she did not take her life in that chair
—no, wait, in this life she did not take her *death*
in that chair

or in any chair for that matter
—she decided to live, in a very big way

—she may have slept in or even with a chair or two
—actually i am sure she slept in and with

—but that is not the big deal her life is
—a bundle, a piece of despair, the world as one rides

or derides or decries it—a map with a nest drawn upon
the wrong country and a few birds and charms in the trees

near them
—and i have sent the general and the colonel (both of whom

had no theme) i have sent them to honor a current teacher,
a little bird who survived Warsville

—a little flu in their heads and trays in their hands
to deliver to the children in real chairs

Take the A Train

*

Take the A Train.

*

once long long long ago
in the someone else sun

*

i cease to kiss Paul Klee
there is nothing rightful about the frog not helping everyone along the
    rock laden road regardless of their motives
i have pictures and picture voices to lessen this account or to make the
    account more
manipulative — you choose!

*

i still have some cards,
some family notes

*

i am the "e" that is missing between Hughes' "Stony Lonesome"
and Creeley's "Stoney Lonesome"

i am the hill where i lived for one week

i am Diane's sun as large as the sun-motive-moon

*

"everything is for K"

"K" who is "R"

if r is k who is r?

*

interview the true zero in your life and see what answers happen on their way
to you

i feel a crime voluntarily entering one of the mailed postcards

*

my dream was crawling onto the train near Warsaw
but it had the wrong train and i tried to tell it so —

as soon as the words were out of my mouth
they began to arrange themselves differently

*

if you are a piano
i am your war-like shoe

"time stumbled and fell" (Szymborska)
and i fell too

one desire
after another

one part of the world at zero force
equaling another part of some part of the unequaled cosmos

*

leaves to
figure to
eye level
to Christ
to subway to
work to heart

*

to i am waiting until
at least 7 pm to take a shower

i could take one now
i am a tree and a houseboat today and both

are out
and out of place

*

i can flounder like a star
said the first star on the horizon
but tonight i will not flounder at all
i will greet both wisdom and straw
as one hand

*

did you have much trouble
tonight coming up in silence
like you did — "coming up" —

*

i came up to the boys but the boys
made me feel like there was a ghost
or something i could not / did not
understand about their house

*

i saw one of their sisters decades later
and what struck me was i recognized her
from yards away— the look she had was even
younger though in some sense everything about
her — her face — her walk — "things" like this—
aspects— were still the same or more notably

*

i didn't remember the books i brought
or the chalk or the money i was to bring
and divide later

*

i didn't remember the ladder or the secure
faces in the boat dream which bordered on
the ditch and the strange barn which flapped
"like an insurance policy" the dream said —
and there was a pathetic wordplay on the word
"premium"

*

am told the stove made a sound by itself
and sometimes in the night went "yes, yes"
like a verbal tic — the window

*

crossed and recrossed herself while
crossing the room —words were to be seen
as suns

*

but you can't see a sun directly

*

hey, where are you now, and which book
are you holding directly up to the sun or
the lamplit room — i didn't remember how
many had gazed at the window but i can tell
you the full name of two students who ran
from her at two different times but ran just
as fast

*

i am not the terrible man you made me out to be
but i am not often very fine either — one thousand times
i wanted success hugely or some other woman or
some other country or house but i suppressed this

*

of course you suppress just so much
and it starts oozing out sideways like your
life is made up of poorly done math or snow
or snow melting or even drool

*

as the sun is an end to "else"
and as the moon and the sea are "quick"

*

these are the moonlit trousers i am holding
he wrote a diary piece called "Moonlight, Trousers"

—today at the beach he hears her say
You are the only panted one on the beach

*

the pants of the violent unfairly dead
flap against the save branch on the computer
and they cost a cumulative billion dollars

*

"to forget we write,
for you or for me"

*

The pieces of my dandruff
are as multiple as the votes cancelled
by the state.

*

and the friend has vanished
this side of a cloud

*

i admit to another cheap piece of envy for wanting
the prize money much more than i let on

*

little field, I won't murder anyone here
if you won't.

*

one, two, buckle the widow's shoe
three / four

close the widow's bank account

*

she was the swiftest widow we had
ever seen and there was something
to the way she closed his door that
was too provocative and too secret
and too ungenerous

*

"After" for Tom —what summer
does not come without your vast echo?

*

(The) Ex Tapes
"She makes money
off of dead people."

*

Cheyanne went west and then was disenfranchised
by the little remaining family (east) she had

*

she had other family, true, but they were only
in a very poor position to help her — and they got
very drunk and left her sometimes — and she had
these stories of living in seventeen or eighteen places
in fourteen or fifteen years

*

she meets Tess in a hospital — they both use
these names (Cheyanne / Tess) only with each
other and give the hospital fake first names —
and they are admitted to the same hall on the same
weekend and it is the same weekend Phyllis is admitted

—brought with resistance from the runway of the local airport

*

Tess stared at Brooklyn

*

dream of walking into the wrong room
and not knowing how to cross myself:

the night is lousy like the moon unable
to forgive herself for another and still another birthday

*

some moments in little flashes but more frequently

*

i have this creepy feeling i am going to continually
misspell something important or say it backwards—
what i am really trying to say is i fear i am too headed
for an evening be it a weekend night or not when i will
be so excited and so out of hand i will be brought like
Phyllis in to a hospital or some facility from some what-
the-hell-in-my-life-will-be-the-tiresome-equivalent-of-
an-airport

*

Cage has those lines about R's paintings that both Tess
and I misheard as "airports to airports, / dust to dust."

Or "shadows to airports / dust to dust"

—which was/ is it?

*

you are the knack in the crazy mig
that fired on the innocent village and
each of the innocents in the village and
now you want me to stand here as if you
have never been mentally defective in the least?

*

you were what the war stood for

*

you always talked about ending it for the "wrong reason"
as if that was the big mistake in the first place

*

you never thought the war itself was the mistake,
the killing, the warwrong you sponsored from the
start

*

from the cocoon of your mig

*

when we were in the basement it appeared
somebody—usually a man— was entering the house

from not just the side wall nearly above us
but from the memory of the side wall too

*

we were terrified

*

i did not have my own chair but one night a week
i could use the chair the older couple used — they would
each make some small room for me — i pretended once to
have a slight fever — it was like a childhood way of being
anonymous

*

it seemed so looking back as an adult to this anonymous world

*

but the world was so young too — the trees were

*

young, the sky was very young, pages went
by very slowly or were introduced to you like
little fairly cheap arithmetic problems or holes

*

the woman is not fat
but is pregnant

a) again
b) for the first time

*

the early moon
rises slowly through

a) binoculars
b) two prolonged branches only the binoculars can indicate

*

oswald shot

a) at kennedy three times
b) at walker three times

*

i was a teenage

a) four
b) foreclosure

*

the widow stole

a) five poems which went nowhere
b) a five piece poem which went nowhere

*

i am fishing at midnight with

a) one or two of six "fishing" friends
b) six of my vertigos

*

Oh, I threw out
so many pictures
and with the pictures
the voices (a / 7 b/ 8)

*

not trusting is as thin as
a 9 or multiples of 9

*

when in the course of human flames
my eyes are stoned but astonished to see
a moment of gentle history and pond grass
saved by the night and various fireflies

—various as pond drops / pond ponds

*

you can never tell
when a man like me
is a tree

*

instead let's walk to chelsea
up 7th and let me hold my jacket
on my other arm even if i need it
instead

*

Can't wonder about his hands,
but Michelle wondered about mine, and let me
know. The artist in Michelle wanted them.
Years later I still see Michelle in a boat,
in the black and white photographs. Still
hear her also telling me just draw,
do it, and doing it in the bedroom of the apartment,

*

Daybreak Book

*

one and six makes seven
makes less on the other side of
the planet we haven't observed yet

*

is there a friend who died there too?

look up the mirror story, maybe this
had something to do with the resonance
of poetry

*

there must be some other way of talking
—we're old now he said

*

a distrusted body
a cake kidding her "like a birdcage"

view of addicted life like a wrong turn —
who was that guy?

*

K. said the cars made a noise like the ocean
and he could hear them like he could hear a year

-a drawing of professors who flunked you K. said
-that would make for a comic subject

but i did the flunking he said and K. said of course

city-scape-with-leaves-windows-holes-underground
box people

*

someone was less a key when s/he lived next door

*

taken for granted like an almost ruined bridge
and then you are upon the bridge — drugs take on
a regional flavor

- the couple experiments and takes on the bridge
and they have funny dreams too — they are able
to approach the dream/bridge

as some ultimate passage — they don't know how to
stay with their own lives but they don't know that —
s/he sings "Jesus" in a long lilt but the voice rises

from beneath a third or fourth window —and even though
the voice rises a few times s/he doesn't get up to
investigate the source or face of the voice

*

Death of nowhere
I am a total me.

("note" found on final blank page
of Langston Hughes' *Collected Poems*)

*

My mother was born in Forest Glen, Nova Scotia, in 1910.
She came to the United States to join her sister Lelia
and she was married to my father Paul Bernard Burkard
in Rome, New York, in 1933.

*

but there is some other way of taking the biography
out to the curb or out to lunch or out to the pines in back
to be buried like some summer treasure one could return to
at some later or much later date

*

the cakes she includes in her installations and sculptures
can (and will!) actually be eaten — they are "real"
cakes

*

am not the elegant universe
i once thought myself to be
or once in a while was thought
to be by someone else or by a

rock or a pond or a fabled frog
—not to be painted now by J. or B.
either — chalk night talks,
erasures

*

sun as soon
to see you soon, yes

*

soon

Thank You

Thank you Rafael Camacho for
your poem "The Charcoal" —
the latter another word I have
never used in a poem.

*

Thank you Jeannie Turner
for "The ticking of the clock"
—I read "While the Clock Ticked"
as a young poet-boy and the book
became a psychological metaphor
of sorts for my sister or more accurately
in my life my brother life.

*

Jorge Robles you close your poem
with "my brother" and I close some
of mine with my brother. Maybe we could
exchange brothers and see if they would
close or open poems. Are you still
writing?

*

Dear Jennie Ortiz,
in the fifth grade I had not written
anything nearing a poem. I wrote

something silly in the next grade
because we had to. When I was
thirty-eight years old I wrote a
poem which had a red horse in
it and dear Nancy —because of
an idea or a wonderful misread
—made the red horse red. Rojo caballo rojo.
Thank you Rojo rojo.
Thank you Jennie.

*

I have heard of "my sister life"
but not "my brother life."
Sunithi told me that when she
grew up in India the moon was
an uncle. I could thank Sunithi
not only for her poems but for
the possibility of "my uncle life."
I have been lucky enough to have
a prolonged "moon life." I use
the word "lunar" too because
I want there to be as much moon
in this as possible.

*

I wrote a poem entitled "Shadow
from Breathing" —it is—not sur-
prisingly —a black and white poem—
not because it is or includes shadow
—a real life one! — although partly
because of that — no it is what i

would call a black and white poem
also for its flatness— a way of seeing
the world for a moment the way
photography would—of course there
are many color photographs too
and color poems—some writers
i realize are almost only one thing
for me—not in any sense of a limi-
tation either—Creeley for instance
is a black and white poet for me—
my shadow from breathing included
fear—it tried for a long time to link
up with another poem which was
a painter friend—Nancy Modlin Katz—
whose paintings are completely color!
—and this linked attempt was also trying
to include some horses and the word
"foal" — i was using the word in a shallow
(not shadowy) way without acknowledging
to myself that shallowness — it is usually
this lack of acknowledgment that threw
the poem or the link to another world
off —there was a piano too—so you can
see just by two of these objects—the foal
and the piano—and of course the foal
and the piano as words—you can see
i was probably overreaching or underreaching
—an acknowledgment of shallowness could
not have hurt—after many half-lifes and
four or five years "Shadow from Breathing"
came into its-thin-and-black-and-white-own.
No Nancy, no foal, no piano—no stranger.
Vilma Mejias writes "Fear" and "Mother Nature"

and fear has a shadow in it as mine does
and then they are thin like my breathing too
often is. i see green partly though when i
see Vilma's poems—i see color—the position
of "nice" in fear and "infants" in the second
poem seem like color places/words.

*

Thank you Miklos Lengyel for writing
"The Beauty of the World" in which a
Mr Bowman appears. I had a bow and
arrow when i was in my first loving house
and the bow fell from the shelf in the garage
and cracked in two—it was a rojo crack which
i never realized until just this moment. it feels
Miklos like i have been fighting with a version
of this rojo crack for an afternoon. The beauty
of the world was that i had a bow and a garage
shelf to drop it from. The beauty of the world
was an awkward half poem about my dear
aunt Dorothy a year after she died in which
i was trying to write something after this image
of her or the rain on stilts wrote itself. i could
take that half poem out of a folder and stop it
right where it stopped writing itself — i made
the night on stilts in a poem or note in a secret
boat i wrote—i obviously have not wanted
these stilts or this bow or this aunt or the beauty
of the world to die. And i did not know this
this way at all until i saw your name and read
your poem.

*

What do I mean by a real life shadow?
I mean a shadow for some of us is more
real in a poem or in a photograph than
in "real" life—or the shadow there draws
my attention to the life—otherwise I would
miss. A real life shadow means a change
also. An element. A form cloud.

*

People are real life shadows too.
Billy Constant wrote "Rivers" and
he writes of the Niger and the Nile
and the Mississippi and the Delta.
I don't think I have ever written of
any of these—I write of some generic
rivers but this can be a problem and
can be fake too. But first I want to say
that as well as a river simply the writer's
name—Billy Constant—shadows me and
my figure Bobby Enchantment. The name
of a marble I wrote about once and actually
have written about other times in notebooks.
What names we have—like rivers— and
names to turn to. And then—no joke—
there is Larry Rivers and Alex Katz and
my friend Pat has a small "Bonnard-like"
Katz which is the one which got him thrown
out of Hans Hoffman's class—Hoffman said
"You may be greater than Bonnard but
not in my class!" and asked K. to leave with

the painting. Pat is pretty sure it is the one
she has. She is / was among them as a
friend. She and I hover around some
constants and I will probably introduce
her or reintroduce her to Billy Constant
and his constant Rivers. I know she has
the book. Thank you.

*

Let's pretend Guy Peters is still writing poems twenty-seven years later
and is doing very well and has published four or five popular collections.
And let's pretend Guy Peters is teaching at X for a week or two and is
reading there also. Let's pretend a "student" named Geraldine has
    dropped by
to talk with me for a half an hour about life and writing and not much
    and mentions
attending Guy's reading. Talks about what he read. One was about a meteor
shower, another about the Tall Ships, another about the trip to Singapore.
Let's assume "the trip to Singapore" is an actual quote of Geraldine's.
The "the" implies the homage she has for Guy. The "the" implies
a suggested dose of homage for someone else, like me. I am not saying
Guy says "the trip," but Geraldine's "the" also implies much of the world
knows of this trip, that the listener, me, should know. There is the shadow
of a "should" in her "the." A real life shadow. A six letter shadow
crowding into a three letter word which is now a three letter shadow.
And that doesn't even include the shadow of tone "should" has.
It's a different tone than "the," but it arrived because of "the" position.
There is a completely other kind of shadow in Guy Peter's untitled poem
which is held in a phrase like "I was a river of dreams." It's as if the poem
is a shadow smasher. It's a prosy shadow smasher, it is even blatantly
about "happy things." The narrator even sneezes near the poem's end.
True. Look it up. Page 157.

*

Thanks to Richard Rivera for writing
"My pen is like a poem-writer.
My pen is like a human being."
A poem-writer is like a form cloud.
It is a word which is a ghost of itself.
A bridge between two ghosts.
Before the ghosts shove out into city life
for an evening or another night or day.
Before a human-writer or a human poem
can locate the strange set of words
which were overheard by a judgment
or by a man-servant or by an animal.

*

Thanks to no one, and to Tracy Lahab,
and to Tracy's "little bug." There was a
miniscule spider wrapping her web down
from the cold tap and it was early—six a.m.
or so and I said there is no way this spider
is going to last here —she is bound to get
bumped and drained. So I took a small
piece of toilet paper and guided the little
dot of her on to it with whatever could string
along and placed her in a world of paper
where she would stand as far as I know a
much better chance of lasting longer. It
occurs to me I may not know and that
maybe I interfered with something else.
But something else might have been inter-
fering with me too, or with the small room,

or the water, and it's endless. Or it's a word
like "endless," infinito, french, yiddish.
A trace of lahab—la habitat. Finito. *Fin* (French for end)

Under One Small Fear

Under one small fear
Under one small leaf
Under one small notecard

Under one small city
Under one small business
Under one metamorphosis

Under one small week
Under one small happy experiment

Under two small deaths
Under two palm trees

Under two silences
Under one turned over gymnasium chair

Under a sixteenth planet
Under a forty seventh moon

I do not know where seventeen countries are
and I cannot name or locate the moons
of other planets

Under one jag
after the jagged fire

Under one jag
after the little written sun

and the sunlight that fell under
the question and under the minute tent

Under the "you are younger" flag
and the flag of school

Under the doctor's script
Under the Vietnamese stone

Under X's exception
and X's mixed sunlight

Under under
Under human flavor and looking back

Under no memory
Under Rose

and under Rose's children
Under Rose's sea-self

and cigarettes
and vertigo's last lamp

Under Charlie's bag
and the eerie but distracted sequence of the horses

Under the pink motel on the pink bluff
Under the visible orphans and the boxes they own

Under my sister and her saving grace
Under my brother and the tender foot of his eyebrow

Under my dog's dog
and my cat's dark

Under the yellow pad of my fish
and the twenty seven closings of the door

Under the counting and the friends of math
Under Cindy and a missing no one

Under Zac's Z
and the smudge of the elf

Under the smudging and the oranges of the no way worker
the worker who was summoned
the worker who had proof

The worker of Avis and the only road to her
The thick worker of Michelle and the countless beams she painted

The those of Marsha and the those counting
Under the tin meaning and the peopled soul

Under proof of vertigo
Under leaving the movie lights—one place was very awake

Under a copyright of sound and a cable to Lester
Under und and unto

Under the missing link
Under the shirt of death and the shirt of Felix

Under the blouse of death and the blouse of Tanya
Under death as two coins

Under the name which went wrong and sideways
like Martha and Will and one of the nameless ones
from the nameless universe of the city

Under what you have stolen and what you have dreamed
Under every shoulder and every envelope

Under the spider and the supreme scent of protein
Under the chart of the house and the marred poverty of the sound

the kept
the head
the deferred equation
the failure to laugh

then with some quite childhood the little corner and the little wave
the algebra of smuggling
the dream of two people who are dreaming about a judge

a localized judge and a localized anesthetic
the original message of the planet Jupiter

Tonio's dream
What the planet Pluto did not say or whisper

Under what occurred to you
and something more

The bag anyway
In front of that out of which hung a fir branch

Hanged versus hung
Some things matter and some things do not matter

Under the matrix of my mother and her way of avoiding me
The necessity of vanishing—and clouds

Clouds for for
clouds for morphic resonance

Clouds for Beethoven and
the seeming stillness as the waves clock

Under the exit and the millionaire drinking milk
Under the child who is walking without any moral law

Under the Chagall and the joke of the single sun
Under the electrician and the hole in the house

Under the bear
and the interests of the forest

Under the panties the child is painting
Under the tree and the too and the truck

Under the umbrella
el paraguas
and the r and the f

Under the k
and the light and the shadow of k

Under how dark the inside had become
your friend's darkness

Under your friend's darkness
most of all

Under the errand the la bota
Under la mano and the clockface

Under the drops a hated child has named
Under nothing named and no names at all

The pages of the window
The alcohol of the drum

Even in the soul you cannot find a picture of the wind blowing through you
Or snow falling on the mouth and the snowface

Under turn your head away
Under the whispers of the anti-birds

Under the ravens
and the river which was higher than the house

Under the shower and the saving dimes
Under the footwork

Under the whole world of rain
Under unforgettable

Under one name
Under one thumb

Under the name which hit you
Under the hand which attempted to paint the evening star

Under e and d
and all hauntings

Under my ghost and your ghost
and all the coins received by ghosts

Under the statue of limitations and the pigeons which shit on it
Under the marsh light and the girl with a tool

Under Szymborska and Fuentes
and Malena's box

Under not anybody
File me "under" "Not anybody"

Under hives
Under pilfering funds meant for public school

Under the channel which awakened at 5 a.m.
and could still be received on Neptune

Under Uranus
before it was pronounced Your-Ah-Nus

Under the circles we are told to draw
and the collaborations for the deep gods

Under stone and wound and lunch
Under Ray's robbery and my favorite Ramone

Under tomb and second and neighbor
Under Lisa and the must life

Under Ken and the bus
Under the dream of carrying a vase of bees

Under moist flowers
Under the poem of the forgotten dog

forgetting to bite me
"There was a Doctor in the Village"

"My Handwriting is Your Handwriting"
My job is to throw parties

Under the parachute
and under the shootist

Under the misreadings
and the breezes that tell the truth

Under the turning of the truth
and the skeleton of the birthday

Under the film and the indecision
Under the orchard and the attributes of the worm

Under the taking of the pencils
and the taking of the waving flag

Under the photograph
Under the splotch

Under the demented beer
the undone "other ride"

Under Ellen and the village of Ellen
the wrist of the place—the flame—

the telephone
the caresses

The memento of e
The swimmers

The bathers
The nudes

II

anger

when you have produced a black flower which ends more than one sentence

when you sit between the wall and the broken face of your own life

when you have hardened because the moon inside you was lost and found
and lost again

when you found your moon a week later in a pawn shop but thought it
was the shadow moon and sold the thing for a hole in the night worse
than you could have dreamt

when you have filed charges against yourself but no one sits at the
appropriate desk to take the paperwork from you

when the black flower ends a sentence before you end it

i remember one day when my eyes touched the day

i was accused of being too elementary in the world

and "furthermore to what purpose is your elementariness" the charges
continued

the next day and the day after that i was forced to read interview in which
i said i loved myself—i was talking in the interview about myself by
name—in third person—my voice was described by investigators as
"pinned to the gills of a fish"

"if you must know" they said—"don't stop reading aloud until we tell
you to" was another thing said as a reminder

my voice wanted to see you darling but you were nowhere to be found

i was glad for that—i would not have wanted you to be found

still i missed you like today—and i tried to hear you in the words
between the words i had to read—sometimes i pretended you must
have written these words for me—as a major joke
i would eventually get

i got angry

i wanted you and the sea to be my lawyers—my representatives—my
guardians at the very least

i still would not mention you by name—but the investigators sensed my
    neediness
they began offering me pawn tickets and pictures of a graveyard they
    said someone very very close to me used to make love in— that this
    "someone" still thinks of that place
a black flower i thought was part of a harmless sentence i had written
    one day was brought to me protruding highly and vulnerably from
    the glass of water i could now drink
what looked like a modern printer under the clock on the wall begins to
    make false starts
what had looked like the moon to me and mine for years the
    interrogators said was no more the moon than a traitor moon—
    a counterfeit—
even my having to read aloud was interrupted over and over by this emphasis
    upon me and my family getting the moon wrong all these years
"it's moon-like" one of them said "it's moon-like like a breast but it is
    isn't the moon — it never was" "even your great grandfather had
    it wrong — the one who grew up in the country — a dolt when it
    came to the moon"
my anger was a day of moonlight i was told
my anger would be printed out for me so i could better hate it and
    myself for what it and i was
a mistake! isn't it obvious the mistake you are! don't you see yourself by
    now! you have heard yourself aloud for almost two days—have you
    heard anything at all!
no i said
i am a nevertheless i said
and i am no longer reading what i have said
i will overtake myself with still another day of moonlight
i will see that no one else is involved—not copper—not a door—not an
    ill house being rained upon by the illness of traitor rain
i will see to it that my unnamed kisser will remain just who she or he
    is—unnamed

no one will have to walk for me and no one will have to witness me
when the evening gets fat or skinny i will make sure the sky senses me
 in the large and the small of my being—counterfeit moon come
 on—come on—
you have never done me harm nor anything less than complete me—
it is to you i remain pledged—knowing who and what you are—knowing
 how fake too i have been in the light inside myself
i will be at last the end of you too
i will be your "face me" and your game of waiting or not showing up at all
i will be the end of me for you
i will leave nothing left for the world to take from me or for the world
 to violate
at the end of the silent evening
at the beginning of the next day
when the moon and the sun act as little stones at either side of the early
 morning womanly world

Another Part of a Non-Witnessed World

What are we/they doing here?

Who is this man, and what has *he* seen? Has he seen me?
   (Ever?)

Is anyone in the hills if we go there?

Did Dave know this peninsula when he painted his peninsula?

What if these drawings and paintings were not signifiers of the world
   but the world itself, only itself, only on to its itness, as in
   I am on to you.

I am on to the fact that the man never did see me, the man above.
   (I am not the man above, I am referring to the man I mentioned
   "above.")

Know now he is dead. I know a story or two about his death. He
   was/is a famous painter and there were some suspicions for awhile
   about his death. He was a very uncomfortable man some of the time.

But what if: Avery's three cows on the hillside are the three cows
   and are the hillside? I know we consider this now and then.
   Sometimes there is a space-alive notion that says this representation
   is the thing, is not the idea.

Black Tree, today, is a garden of Eden and a hanging tree.

There are no witnesses. I comes too long after the fact to be a witness.
   But in alive-time I am a witness. Michelle Cliff's essay
   "Poetry is What Is Reaching out to You"
   informs me of these new world concepts, time-alive, space-alive.

Seated Blonde is seated blonde

— it is my sister-in-life's birthday. She lives near something like
   Avery's *White Sea*.

March in Red makes me want to spend March in bed. It isn't even here
   yet. Nor is *Sunset*, two hours off, three hours off…

I will take two boats and make them secrets...

Avery's *Dark Forest*. Don't want this dark forest anymore.

Once you get to the sea it's like all the witnessing in the world
    starts up.

Anti-Memoir (Moon Death)

I don't remember anything.
You don't either.
I have no idea what we said
to each other, to one another,
to ones like or unlike ourselves.
You don't either, except for the old
white version of this you cling to.
May as well call it Moon Death.
That's what you've done all these
decades. Moon Death. Equivalent
to that. History written by white
male liars, preferably educated,
preferably un. Moon shrieks.
Moon branches to whip the truth
into shape. I don't remember
anything. But now I remember
Moon Death. You got it.
I remember. You're done.
On your way to being done.

Biography

Picture of writer
when young looks like
my writer friend J. when
he was younger — he is
younger by far than
writer on cover—both
though have a moonpatch
partly over each face —
one you can see and the other
you cannot — unless you look
like i did now into the
face of the unassuming and
unkept by fake loan or star
writer

can't meet the wind

let's see: i can't walk into your
apartment because you have the flu /
can't meet the wind because the field
is so wet i would sink in mud /
can't make sight of the deer without
maybe spooking them / the dot before
my eyes / the rain on the windshield /
simple grey band of a ring / i bridge
a very tired face she has from working
too long and drinking too much and now
her farmer uncle is staying with her
for two days / it is her complaint
not mine /

Cease Notebooks

When she informs me all my schooldays are done,
scolded, colded, ruined: when she informs me all
my schooldays are done it is within this moment
I more or less begin to imitate an image. An image
of myself which hasn't even quite formed yet, never
will "quite form." On the melancholy side of a sail,
more or less against the ocean, never standing still
just long enough to be called milk, or shoes. No name
fast. Gates. A small unlikely poorly painted white
fence which still houses or protects some of the small
same insects (all insects are small Mr. Michael) it did
when you (I) crawled from one hemisphere of your (my)
brain to another. I don't care for the two-three-or four
instruments which cracked in the chemistry class. I don't
object to the passive objectivity of corridors patrolled
by thugs. But I protest the asshole teacher, in all her
ravine clothing, instructing the weakest among us to now
"Cease notebooks! Cease notebooks!" Before the glass or
shouts had left one of us in his or her shame. Before
we were bandaged like child-suitcases which had been swimming
for very immature reasons. Before we speared our clothes
to the house. Made to. Unpacked by. Emptied of.
Don't tell me.

— for Gerry, and for Lenore

Cherry Eye

when elizabeth bishop painted
INTERIOR WITH EXTENSION CORD
she must have realized in some untoward
unconscious fashion or semi-consciousness
that i who finally came to read her poems with
excitement when i finally read them as a sister
writer instead of a member of some intelligentsia
if that is the word for it—when i finally read them
then a few days later was not in any way heading
to maryland for my second sober anniversary without
her white covered sunburst book of collected poems
on my lap under my arm in my hands under my awkward
pen as i wrote excitedly some lines besides hers or in
the margins or the white spaces of the page=dreams
—she must have realized that years later a reader / fan /
writer in his/her own rite would look to enter this
interior from the suggested door from the mountain
heaping flower side door to look up once in the interior
to see the extension cord from that vantage point as
a spider web of sorts not that she painted it at all that way
but it looks like the beginning of something aligned
partly with the wall-meets-ceiling line and the slight
"hooks": visible holding it in place to wall and ceiling
looks like a day to start something or keep starting something
not to end something like a writer's life even when he/she
feels the invited or uninvited call of the so-called end

a cloud of dusk

i can't see anymore
i missed every Memphis angel
because of the because clauses—
one night sleeping with two cats
Big and Little
and i am serious about these names
i had a vision reading a John Irving book
i did not want to read never presumed i would read
more than a few pages
there were hallway lights and people's voices
shivering through a downstairs window
i could not put the book down either
even though i literally wanted to put it down
sometimes—i hate that word—i went to a meeting
nearby and i was accidentally or coincidentally on this street
so much i began to think maybe i belong here
i kissed the back of someone's hand
i kissed the hand when it turned back to me
i made sure no page was facing me when i read
and that no one would see what i saw or feel what i felt
i am on a drive where a mirror has collapsed
i want to ask someone else without sight

Construction of a Building

in the house there is a sideways k
and a sideways j and a sideways p

—each is about to be sawed off to
make room for other functions—

sideways because they are about
to be sawed some — not in half exactly

either—they are your application
and your supplication for emotion

of any kind—just take the dust
and the shavings with you when

you leave—will you do this to
night too, unto night

Copy Book

because of the over-priced house i will not buy
because "truly" is not a symbol for anything or anyone
because someone said it would be and this is one of those lost roads
because everyone has a multiplicity of lost roads among their lives
because the houses on these roads over-priced or not
are usually better left as people you wave to
people you feature only in waves

because the moon is not the ragged experience the tree branches suggest
because the tree branches are not here simply for my benefit
because you can save what you don't know about someone
like you can save some money but in the end it will do just about the
    same good
because so many people don't have money you are saving suffering
you are keeping score with a siren
your portfolio is a knickknack of collapsed chairs

Crossdreamer

Pat and I are talking about the past.
I tell her about Tomas Tranströmer's poems
and "The Blue House" in particular. Pat
hears his name in the café wind as Tomas
Crossdreamer. She says it once or twice
before I hear what she is saying. And I
tell her even as I correct her that she is
right, her hearing is right, he is a crossdreamer,
that describes something about him and his work
I had never thought of and never would have
if it hadn't been for Pat and Tomas and the wind.
I tell Malena that same night —it was last night—
she thinks this is amazing too—this new word
now, this new concept. I am late for the next
a.m.'s meeting but I take the book on Mary Hackett
to show C. who is struggling Mary's painting
The Big Me Standing in My Way. I want to give her
the book or loan it but she says no everything
disappears in her house as if it is in a black hole—

I tell her that's okay, she can keep it for a long time —
she says no, really "You won't see it again." But
she looks at the painting and looks and looks.
Not before too long I have this old feeling maybe
I am the one who is supposed to look at this painting,
the big me in my own life, the mental me, the memento
me (hey perfect —me-men-to) — no wonder I had mis-
spelled it for years a momento — as if it was uno momento—
or give me uno momento more — as if by talking about

my poem "A Raincoat" again I could become both a
crossdresser and a crossdreamer — as if the difficult rain
had nowhere else to fall. Sometimes when I go away
from myself it might be that I am going to myself in a way
which I do not recognize at all. I really wanted C to keep
the book also for my poem which closes it, it talks to
Mary, it's about the moon, it is child-like to me, it wrote itself,
but I am beginning to sense a wanting of something else
in this connection to C. As if I could be the rescuer again,
something particular about me, but this is something not
to trust when one is hiding it or unaware it is sitting on
the back porch like a dog which won't return home
until you feed the dog something you don't really want
to feed him.

Can't duplicate Pat's wonderful hearing today
even if I tried. In Mary's "Big Me" there's a "Dog Died"
gravestone to the right of the bridge before the bridge
begins. It's just a few feet from the empty bottle.

Dating to Death

His name had just the right ring
to it, and although you did not
look for his poems right away, you
always thought of him as genuine
because of his name. You were al-
most saving his poems for some
latter day when you did need a
saint. You would hear his voice
then. But it never happened.
You couldn't get a feel for his
work. His name still rung true
but you also knew inside the
crazy stories about his crazy
behavior were getting to you
—they were more boring to you
than anything else, boring like
persons, not stories. Still
you looked, but you saw so much
smartness you felt no sense,
you sensed no feel. Then he
died and you still didn't feel
anything. Sometimes you think
it's you. Dating to death,
treating people like chrono-
logical rings on a tree for
your math and your ear. Walking
in an enchanted forest but
insisting it's bramble land,

and somewhere outside the
forest, when you get the relief
you want, you will realize
you are in Zerosville.

displaced

I should have been Elizabeth
and an only child. Had my mother
had her way. Instead my father
named me (and had his way with her).

I know I shouldn't
but I'm unraveling in fours:
space, time, time, space,
jetlag and numbers of siblings displaced.

My mother asks me
if I would come live with her
when I come back...

Equal but True Story

Dave has done a pear
box— the pears leave
the earth—another
family of delicate
pears is taking from
each other in human
dysfunction—pears
also enter a night
sky in deep space—

the inside of the box
is an equal but
different story. The
pear tree falls from
one wall to the other
on the inside

Fargo, North Dakota

In a small living space,
putting envelopes and
necessary mail in an old
white three drawer bureau
—mail with socks, jockeys
—there's also an unused
electric toothbrush—the
disparate moments of these
things, the anything goes,
has me seeing Aunt Nellie's
drawer in a poor house in
Nova Scotia—things were
just here and there, and
when asked to go find some-
thing for her— and she often
asked — one would see these
assortments that had no high
point except for the fact
of differences. What to
say when mostly the socks
and envelopes and jockeys
invoke a sea of sight—life
there then —Nellie gone on
who knows where —she dis-
appeared last November
just before her birthday.

The Green in the Sun

Walking past the window house where
friends used to live/ reading the small
signs of slogans in the window again /
having forgotten them for the fifth or
sixth or as many as I have remembered
them times / today was a brief misread
which i'm doing a lot of lately (the years
and the eyes or the lack of eyeglasses,
remember) (but i'm walking / who needs
them) / the misread interest / the slogan
sign reads try on the shoes of an enemy
and see how they fit/ i read it for a sec
as try on the ghost of an enemy and see
how it fits/ as i write this i wonder if
it said notice how they fit/ which is cer-
tainly a much different feel than see be-
cause see leaves possibility the shoes or
the ghost won't fit even as i assume now
you're reading ghost (or ghosts if you want)
as an equal or better possibility than shoes
—it's saul's house/ keith and susan and
ellery as a baby lived there a long time
ago / it was a cold winter then just before
susan had the baby/ earlier jennifer and
me are talking about don sterton don was
helpful much to me/ we're talking too about
hey let's go and rescue some lives today of
course that's a joke / to wear the ghost of
an enemy of course would be interesting/

writers' magazines would say i am telling
you things instead of showing you/ as if
that matters / and of course i may be try-
ing to tell myself something too or maybe
a ghost/ today i wonder if the ghost of
an enemy is the same as the ghost of a
friend/ don is a ghost a friend / i would
wear him / i would be honored to wear him
—i am honored that peter and others have
a piece of my sobriety whether they want
it or not! / i want to listen in in the shade
on this very hot day farther up the small
street to the talk i hear the artist giving
the group of students at the henry hensche
school/ i stand in the shade and peer in
through some leaves / i love this/ i overhear
her tell the students a few things and then
she points out something about someone painting
something yesterday and also what winslow
homer or henry would do/ local color is talked
"about" for a moment and then she says that
a cool green creates the green in the sun /
she may not use the word create / but the
green in the sun / what an idea! / what a
statement! / all because i have told jennifer
i will take a tiny jog in the shade / all be-
cause i have made an awkward purchase of
my life/ all because of the poor cat which
was dead in the woman's walk/ all because
of the green in the sun as far as i know/
the shoes and the ghosts of my enemies/
my friends / my windows and every single
stranger out there in the awkward world

Has

not necessarily —
has dated, interviewed
          *

Jack's mind
jinx book
          *

one-wheeled house
ho done it
          *

builds accounts
white rose, stage door, street/coast
          *

fur/anger
ration's voice
three month last
          *

delicately possessive not just a high price
ash-moon, fast-moon, hyphen-moon (i see it! i see it!)
how-is-moon
fish-moon, list me a dove was, pay a finally
know true
some everything with speed and low road for wardless
          *

books are fences
who-done-it some mistake gated stone fence past's
dream time keeps lock in gate
stone/wood each possible

between large car wrist

I Decided to Eliminate All the Eights

in one card game, the eight dominated too much,
and looked like a fat ball too. I decided to eliminate
all the eights. Then, my friend said "I would like to
do away with all the sixes, they are fat in their sack
like I am." I said you are not fat in your sack. My friend
said "I was at one time very very fat." Green is the color
of all eights which have retreated to the corner of the
famous museum and approaching them are their soon
to be loyal soon to be friendly fat in the sack sixes. I send
too many people too many gifts over too many years which
I would have been better off keeping for myself for at least
awhile. I gave up a piece of myself in order to suffer and to
stay still over small human affairs. I wonder like a glove
on a wire outside a rooming house of some discreet ambition
How did I get here, what am I doing, and when will I get off?

I Do Self Portraits

Carol reminded me strongly
of Karen. Karen eeked out
a living 500 miles away.
A man ate his hat.
I can't tell the story the way
Carol or Karen would like
me to, nor can I reconcile
the radio abandoned in the train station
with the rose in polluted waters.
My arm waved at George before I did.
Loneliness is as hard as a horizon.
A crack house no one waves from ever.   (EVER).
Two months later I'm unbeknownst,
on Carol's street, in Karen's
lilac, in rain.

"I have a yellow heart"

Y de tanto no responder　　　　　And from offering no answers,
tengo el corazón amarillo.　　　　I have a yellow heart.

— "Another," Pablo Neruda, translated by William O'Daly

I have a yellow heart.
I have an "I" in my yellow heart
Her heart was much bigger
It had an eye

When I was falling out of my childhood
like one falls out of a car
Likened to a breathless sentence
the man who remembered and hated the man

who owned the mean dog
began to tell
at a table beside
these two yellow hearts— "I" and eye—

a bigger day could not have formed a river
unless the day had been able to sneak up on night
like an old misspelling
a cataract belonging to of course a cat

found in the metropolis
nursed back to help
living a slightly amputated but meaningful life
a lame yellow

memory when it eats the mint of nobody
or someone who is too far
too fat
for his own good

Still I have a yellow heart
In a moment of personal cowardice
I will telephone the housesitter
to distract myself

from my own more real story
more real than the one I tell
In another moment
I will desist

and name some early conflict with math
as the result of an unwanted and unexpected
conflict with god
with sledding

With climbing the heights of this yellow
Here where one is already a third or so dead
it is important to point out
that by yellow I do not mean to imply cowardice

Indeed I imply a brightness
a simplicity and a radiance
a power
a helping hand too — and an "eye"

always an eye within—
One time she said to me she would turn up
in another's face
framed in a train window

or in a photograph come upon
in the face of still another
and another
like the stars at night—

This is one math problem
I should have paid more attention to—
to the phantom who wore the hat
which was borne away by the sea wind

—or was it a chime?
or was it a name you had never heard of
an abbreviation
or was it that forgotten house

where since
tells its own stories
whenever since wants
and with whatever emphasis since desires.

In the Direction of the Sea

— for Tomas Tranströmer

I was one of the silent ones
but I had to talk because
you were much more silent.
Walking in silence was for
uncountable reasons not
bearable. Frequently I look-

ed sideways while talking
because the sea was there and
the spaces between the houses
were frequent and I must have
thought if I went into that
sense of space where I could

make up for the silence.
In the direction of the sea
I was not making up any-
thing, and oddly, *because*
of all this discomfort,
probably not making anything

up either. Our clothes
were faces we hadn't even
imagined yet. Some friends
started to come near but then
thought better of it. Fre-
quently you looked sideways
in the direction of the sea

lucky coat anywhere

I have four green roads to show customs
my father is transforming himself into a wife while I am playing cards
    with him

I is a leaving and a point of reference
only the opposite of lust is in the child's face in the mirror

my dog eats away at my central mirror and I know this is not true
a few men deceive me like your ghost and your destination

the one in motion is uncut love
uncut Rilke and the fluttering of him (Rilke)

defeat this water and this door and this view of the door
the road is a white fine while they interview you

you are an I among many
a lucky coat anywhere

sex is green a spoon a question
shape of deliberate clay and places of trees

original compound places
this fluttering glass from the prison window

a six of clubs
something

a ten of diamonds
a detective of agriculture who has killed the smallish farmer

small fathers were beaten by books and by moonlight
books died by hand

Rilke was unborn
but an umbrella was needed

The Man

— for John

said he had been painting
since three or four a.m.
and because I did not know
whether he was painting a house
(I didn't think so but you never
know) or painting inside the house
as in a studio his own I decided to
ask him: and I asked him with some
excitement because I secretly hoped
he would be infected by my enthusiasm
would want to talk would show me his
art and I would show him mine (I don't
show hardly anyone): he did not seem
taken aback but seemed cold or maybe
mildly threatened then too it was pretty
early in the day when I asked him the few
times I have unexpectedly bumped into him
during the day in this town or in the next
he seems to always be friendlier at ease
with me as I probably am with him: there
isn't any time for a secret there or for
a hidden agenda which could cast a shadow
this way and that for a good long period.

Mathematical Angel

Don't have any proof of this.
Do have rain,
things around the room: a harmonica
(blue and small),
a photograph of you much too far
away, lamp, desk, tapes,
shoes, memories of shoes, papers
from various stores and receipts
to draw upon or write upon,
algebraic tables which appear
obsolete, sunlight which is
hastening rain's end and obsolete
memories, —this is not where
I was headed.

Milieu

January: interesting to see the corpse light that, so oddly lovely, there in peace. Had never seen (or it is felt once) that before.

January: one is forever an ending. Woods, clouds. I could have said woods about the corpse. One can see through.

January: to use maps of the world: in this country and in other countries children and women (these as always in particular) are being shot at like memory is shot at in discussion of ideas among those not on the line but probably on line, like memory of those who have never been shot at.

January: point isn't that they don't shoot. Identities find walls and ears and arms missing. One corpse is rolled over to see what page of light to identify the corpse by now.

January: rites ending. My temple. Breath. A migrant moon.

January: not going to make a faith of an echo. But one is given a mirror. One is given a ghost. One will give up only the forgiveness: the rain, the woods, the clouds, the breath of a friend.

January: John and I seeing something by sea's surface that maybe we were not meant to see. We mention his face after two decades. We don't want to talk about it or walk about it. The Coast Guard house literally in harbor at Provincetown, waiting out rough weather/winter before being "shipped" to Race Point.

January: camera. Window. Small glee to see Grace in Chelsea window. Windows where I could come from is the thought. Windows I know in a heart's eye, a heart's ear.

The Military

I woke up this a.m. and I felt
lousy—lonely too. In one dream
it was my turn to talk at a
12-step meeting, and just as I did

more than half the people got up
and left. Fifteen minutes is a lot
to a flea. But how would I know
for sure? I said I was a success

story. I didn't take credit, I spoke
of other hills and vistas. Maybe
my tone was lonely. I also dreamed
that frogs who knew I loved creatures

so much they would simply attach
themselves to me when they saw me
coming —and a lovely very smallish
green bird alighted on and off from

my finger as I walked around a town—
this was lovely and light but then the
dream had a slight portent sense to it
—and when I emailed this portion of

the dream, to two friends, I closed
with the joke of "a broken record poem"—
then the dream had a slight portent
sense to it/ then the dream had a slight

portent sense to it/ then the dream...
Soon you won't be able to sound like a
broken record. You can't sound like a
broken tape, or a broken CD, or can you?

The Moon Nude

Saw Don today—he said i looked gloomy. I did.
Two hours before I was Mr. Ungloom. Now my shirt
even worked against me. My eyes behind my darkest glasses
could not stay still. I looked for legs, faces. I forgot where one stair was
but nothing happened to me. I played a public piano standing up. I wondered
—almost aloud really—how could I have spent literally all my youth in my
        father's house
with his organ of one brand or another there and not understood—until
        my 40's?—that
you can do a lot with one hand just hanging around a small number of notes—
much of this is just in the variation. A couple walked by the other side of
        the room
and looked over at me. I went from playing just the black keys—the half
        notes—
to just the white keys—I often have more trouble hearing the white keys—
I don't know why—I don't get them as well—but today, June 11, I got
        something
I usually don't get.

One day in Manhattan— it was twenty years ago in another June — I was
        leaving
my job at noon at Bloomie's to get to St. Bartholemew's —St. Bart's—on
        Park and
50-something. Friday was always a speaker meeting. The room always felt
        special
that weekday. L'incontro intimo for some reason. These things like getting
        the white keys
are hard to explain. Or there simply aren't any —it isn't the right notion
        to begin with.

It's a session not with a nude but with the moon nude. Or the moon
　　　nude over the big city
—bright and full at the literal end of Houston Street—nude to the extent
　　　that there are
no shadows anywhere, or there may as well not be.

But it is one day now—it is a Friday—nothing dramatic is going to happen
　　　—but I am running
slightly to get to the meeting, then walking fast. I am just about to come
　　　past a fancy hotel
on Park when I realize John Irving is waiting out front and looks like he
　　　is dressed to start
jogging. I knew John slightly in Iowa City, and later in 1981 he is going to
　　　read at the Fine
Arts Work Center in Provincetown. But that is another story. I want to
　　　tell it in something
called "Paper Moon." Wait for me.

When I stop to say hello to John he is standing still but I start jogging in
　　　place. Running
in place. I intentionally frightened my brother so much rising up hidden
　　　from a couch
as he crossed the room that he ran in place. I am not frightened but I am
　　　running in place.
He is standing still. I am glad to see him. He seems glad to see me. I
　　　mutter something
clear and wanting to about my not having the best attitude when I saw
　　　him last in
Provincetown. It's called envy with a capital E.

We both have to head on so we do.

I get to St. Bart's. You had to take an elevator to the second floor room
    for the meeting.
I always liked to sit in back. Today —this Friday in June in 1984 — I
    imagine Elvis — or
as I really enjoy more calling him still — I imagine Elvis Presley
    qualifying —telling us
his story. What we used to be like. What happened. What we are like now.

I have him for some reason wearing a red shirt which is bold and demure
    at the same time.
He tells a good story.

We know each other a little bit but we aren't close friends in the
    fantasy—don't have to be.

It is good to see him and to hear him.

It is not a day of a riderless horse. It is a day of a horseless rider.

It is very okay.

The sun is out.

The moon is still nude.

Moonstruck Alone

This is the painting which my brother
Paul Klee never completed—I make use
of its redbird on rainy mornings like
today, when I hear my train say "You
can tell me," but you are *5*, a *23*,
a locust tree touch decided to hide upon
for a few more minutes, and the miles
are mysterious facts which arrive un-
announced like night mail, Charlie
telling me to follow the witness in
the windows of the metropolis, Malena
knowing this is only a bad minute children
ask for, and, in any case, it's better
than Dante whispering, balloon-like,
unlike his miniature body squeezed between
your birthday and mine. It's difficult
to say why you are *m* and I am *n*, there
may even be an insincere zeal in bringing
this up so publicly. But we're leaping,
buying shirts and light bulbs for the
long stay, I desire love of you and no
clocks, no syntax or tailor who really
chooses our color on Tuesday, but because
we waited until Saturday, you can trust
me, you can tell me, and no one but *b*
can talk to me with your wing.

Mr. Faceless Meet Mr. Face

The hill was a yellow.
The guy kept coming upstairs to take your picture.
Eventually people thought you were having an affair.
There was one secret-woman-friend
one secret-man-friend.
They knew each other but not that you knew both of them.
Both of them were like the hill and the other guy:
the other guy helped you look down on life so you could look
into it. Not for answers but for wondering.
There were no answers.
One man worked in a closet. This became his answer.
But he told you just this summer that he rejected that.
The pictures the guy took wound up upon another friend's
stairway attic step. In a shoebox, in assumed dark, in
assumed sale of house, now sale after sale, year after year,
sea after sea, flat interior landscape which once was sea or
almost sea. Mr. faceless from sea after sea meet Mr. Face
from almost sea. The two of you have this rare opportunity
to not only meet but maybe get to know each other. Not every
face meets a face, or every facelessness a face.
Hill meets yellow, yellow makes hill
one secret-man-friend makes one secret-woman-friend.
Summer meets answer. You meet summer in assumed dark.

My Nickname for Darkness

Overheard voices.
But I am overhead,
so the voices are
more overheard by

the summer night
wind than by me.
It would help if you prayed
said my name for darkness.

Anyway, it said, it is time
to leave me alone: the moon is slanted,
the night is not long
but it isn't short either.

There is a tale to tell.
We both have one.
And a period, a "with,"
a so-called envelope

to send a so-called letter
to someone who might listen.
But we suspect, don't we,
more and more, that the

someone or the other someone
isn't listening like she used to,
or like he used to, and in this
there is nothing strange or obscure.

The Nude Moon

One time on a day when hardly anything but the sun and blue sky were out
the moon decided to visit the library and look up a book called CALDER IN
CONNECTICUT. The moon had recalled entering a big bookstore and
    waiting
for a long time for someone who had not yet known how to experience her.
While waiting the moon took to sitting in a big moon chair with these funny
pictures of—yes—Calder in Connecticut—inside and out. And then—
    two days
later and a night before this day when hardly anything was out—a Calder card
comes in the mail for the moon—and it did not take nearly as long to
    reach the moon
as you would think. But the light wasn't so good—and the moon spent
    part of the night
and day thinking the card represented some circle art by someone named
    Ceravolo
or something close to that. Letters in print and not the sound. And then
    the moon saw
in the very bright sunlight that it was Calder, not Joseph (that was the
    other mistake)
Italian or Joseph Anybody but Alexander Calder (where Joseph ever even
    came from
would be more of an oddity if the moon did not consider what even her
    own "mooniness"
can do—a shadow can appear of course not necessarily more real but as
    interesting as
the real—the dopple of a tree can topple like a book for a moment—a
    love letter
can be sent late and still arrive the day before—or arriving the day spring
    or love began

the letter can bear its fruit like shadows—one thought can follow one of
    the lovers and
then the other —the moon can appear nude—this nude moon
    participates—one lover
proverbially becomes the other not only in shadow but in the day of
    sunlight as well.
The nude moon could be said to be herself il gioco dell'amore. La trasfigurazione.
As the moon does not say "no" there is no il no in amore. Either becomes or.
Or becomes either.

The moon wants to draw a horse. The moon is looking among many examples
for ideas. The moon wants to ride the drawing of the horse past the insects and
the elephants and the tigers and the giraffes and the birds and the fish and
    the mice
and the fice (a new rodent) and the ocean and many stars. The nude moon
wants to ride this horse for as long as there are horses and roads and moonlight
upon such horses and roads.

"Off-key," "Off-keel"

If a poem begins with
lithium or some other
bipolar remedy, you will
walk into the poem and you
will walk out, as simple
as that. Even if you take
a flower with you of mari-
gold proportions. Even if
you are sabotaged with clues.
You yourself will later be
poeticized when least expecting
poeticization—a messageness,
a ness-ness will overtake or
overrun a dream or two—
lighthouses will appear with
bells with a time of day
imprinted on these like a schedule—
you will feel "off-key," "off-keel,"
you will talk in your sleep
before you drop you.

One Day

One day my window was darkened by a train vertically.
One day my wonderful window darkened with gloves.
One day my window darkened with window #44.
Spelling darkened my window on Tuesday, and Wednesday it rained.
One day my window dark drove straight to the bank.
One day I fed the bee-hive from this side of the window.
When I looked in another window the day was not mine, not ever it said.
With their choppy seas, their willingness, their windows.
The ghost of your mother sobbing in the back seat.
Every window has a ghost, but not every car.
Don't come to the silhouette as a confidant.
A cloud would have folded over the hushed harbor but the boaters
    had mad pasts they wanted others like us to hear. We would have to
    stay in late and suffer their voices. Skipping is such a false name
    for such an activity you said.
You said your window isn't the only one which is darkened.
I haven't been alone for two years.
I can't sit still with myself, if that is who I am with.
One of the poets wrote whatever stupid thing I may have said or done.
It was the unwillingness to be stupid which kept me away, or what I saw
    as the unrelenting unwillingness to be stupid. But I don't finally
    believe in my sources any more than I believe in the poet's.
One of the windows is something my dream said is much older.
My dream of day.
My confidant boards the train three towns after I do.
I say I do in the windowed dark of a wet book.
Against what tree have sticks lashed at blue windows?

My child has been driven out from still another town and is about to
  eat the hands of his little watch.
If the window gets caught taking another window, reach in your pocket for
  a rock, a fork, a piece of literature you can drape on a tee shirt
  when the street in the world feels like you must have wanted
  something.

Paintings of Hours

I have this image of you as a waif. I have beside
me MY HORSE AND OTHER STORIES by Stacey Levine. I
see you and your hours and your horse. I see your
paintings of hours and of your horse. Under Levine's
book is a book by Lyn Hejinian, WRITING IS AN AID TO
MEMORY. I haven't read the book yet, I love the title.
But I am not sure whether I buy the title or not; of
course, I don't know if Hejinian buys it either. I
love the fact of both books deeply, I love the thing-
ness of them, them as objects—and as worlds to an-
ticipate me. Perhaps I/we anticipate them. Who knows?
the island in me says. The sketch in me says. Tomas
Tranströmer's sketch, and bookcase, and made-up but to
me oh-so-real-ghosts; Tomas' island, Tomas' blue houses.
And the sister life in me says so too, I love these
these worlds-yet-to-come, these worlds where much will
easy and in plain sight, and you can make your way
safely from home to school and back again without being
bombed or bombed into orphanhood or lack-of-a-tribe-hood,
lack of a city- or a moon- or a sun or a river-hood.
Lack of a hood-hood. Pasternak's sister life, Tomas'
sister life, now Maria Flook's sister and sister life.
All sisters want to become real I write (Tomas had written
—in one translation—*all sketches want to become real*)
I am a tired drawing, but a drawing nevertheless. I wonder
if you are drawing today, painting. I feel like I brought
both calamity and joy into your life, our life. Many
other states and feelings in-between.

Portrait of a Man Who Drowned
Wearing His Best Friend

What does the space mean
when covered over with another
half space of agony? How to hint
at your own consciousness when

the dead like the sun in the song
or the sun on the cartless road
first thing in the first morning?
The waterfall in the Hollywood

movie one did not look back to
until one said to one's self
my life is like this movie backdrop
too. And my life is like the forest

I have abandoned for the self,
and the creek on the way to the
forest, and the porch the river
makes before it is poisoned near

the sea, and the birdsong which
is a multiplicity like children are
and rain is a friendship and
I won't look at you again

in the same way
I promise.

— for Patrick

A Recovery Artist

Kafka's Gregor's sister "was of contrary opinion."
Some investigators bring other contraries: a sister
wants to rail against a sister, a mother against a lost son
—the sun very much against the moon in the feeble insomnia
the writer has mailed to another writer, a recovery artist
mailing chapters to recovery artist, the black letter of a
Z among other black letters and numbers and diagrams
in an old notebook. Am I not myself if I am contrary to language?
Am I not myself as some dog you painted? But you must not do
too much, stand too long, caretake too long when one should be
standing like myself beside the brick of the school wall,
the elementary school in the elementary evening, waiting
the arrival of the lost brother to convince him at last of his bad memory,
his devotion to something he knows not yet, something
physical and spiritual and sudden like insomnia— at the same time
waiting for his closeness whether it is "to you." Tell him his closeness
could be for the sun or the moon and it would not matter—
you can even tell him you passed an old friend and something came back
     to you—
tell him it resisted closeness but seemed like it wanted to be of that current.
No box of recovery. No rearranged rider. No ghost behaviors. No umbrella.
Tell this brother of yours you are now his sister, the end of a letter in the
     end of a
tree at the end of the block. Your wings are real, in the shapes of Z and *if.*
There is no prior melody or rejection. Your wings are his wings. Tell him.

Seven

This is not a good number.
For starters, it doesn't really know much
about pain. Erasures, yes. Pain
and these half-drawings which
appear in her books—no.

No, never — did you think pain
actually wanted to be just
that—what if it wants out too,
like we do, what if pain wants
to be the cut figure from your

story darkling, the eliminated,
the *I'll see you later* discard
who turns up in sleep a few
imagistic years later, years
without tone, years where we

de-split, waving like the tail
of who said which comet, I say
the one we can't quite see,
with seven kisses elliptically
roaming the inner and outer

glacial galaxy, a mistake and
not, a kiss for darling and not,
a kiss which is a history, a
life past, a tone fed.
Woods too: no good, no bad.

Six

I told someone I was taking *six*
like a number for life and death.

Table. Decree.
Wind shatters simple year-sound

in photograph. I say seriously:
if you love photography the way

you say you do, and I believe you
the way I say I do, then take six

photographs of the cover of Laura
Jensen's *Bad Boats*, the book of

poems with yellow waves on the
cover. Six photographs looking

at it on a table from different
cover-angles, or five with one

photograph for the inscription you
say Tess wrote, something like

"I am putting on my overcoat now
and heading out to take a walk."

Did she say that to me, write that
to me? Book found after these years

by your telling me?

Six Fives

Often is not a character,
despite what you said.
"Sleep with the fishes"
not the suspicious command
you imagine it to be.
You imagine you much more
suspiciously and cogently:
a life spent inside a mirror,
endless punctuation, leaves
unspelt upon the nearby
lawns and hillsides. Someone
else's voice in an irrefutable
fact, irritated, iridescent.
Neither the voices of a shadow
nor the voice of a subject.
Someone as an object. One
wing of a maladjusted angel.

Stone's Staircase Collage.

What are you doing in the perfect suitcase of Kansas?
Surely you are climbing slowly because you are genuinely
old, your cane is also genuine, your moving aside for

someone else to pass you is true also. But library
stairs can collapse under such dalliance. The door
at the top is audible instead of open. Your dad

is a surprising current somewhere near — stone, ledges,
etc. Disappointment in breathing. Write down…
Slab isolates woman with can at ledge slab top

man and unknown person have made an iffy old mistake
mistaking a lock for a window and slab side.

string theory

sometimes when i see her she starts
a response to something simple with
what feels like it is going to be another
long story—or if not long too long for the
circumstances of these infrequent crossings—
and i am not alone in this — don't' get me wrong
or right for that matter — i have overheard her
accomplish this tedium with everyone else around—
but it really isn't tedium—it is something wrong in
the context of the setting —someone with this
story energy and matter of fact way could be
holding people riveted instead of at bay if the
constant context was not this infrequent crossing—
string theory, the war according to her eighty year
old uncle, the recent poetry lecture which was
another shot to the head with a pistol of inordinate
accurate dullness— i bet when she is in the wild
field walking her dogs as i know she does she is
in the grips of something far more interesting—
like wonderment about the present moment only
and how the wind seeps into the ground as well
as people in its ordinary and endless way—but end-
less isn't really the right word for this—more like
sometimes or even never if you want to object to
this idea as i am beginning to also

Sun Layers

My arms rise—
this is partly because
I am standing in front
of someone else—

so close their arms
could look like mine
from far away—
and from as far away

as the sea I am afraid
of I could take to the streets
with these arms intact
if something deadly

or wounded
should happen to mine.

Sun Layers (2)

Gee but I'm lonesome.
Gee but I'm out of sentences.
Bee but what happened to my bus poem.
Gee we destroyed his bicycle
    as if it were a secret.

How do you destroy a secret.
How did you come upon that answer:
How does your "love/hate" syndrome
    align itself with "pass/fail."
How did the boats do.

Somone is looking for me
the way I used to look for myself.
It is possible to find me.
I found me.

Talking to a Fragment

She used only a yellow, a blue, and a lime in the drawings.

He wanted to walk into the Scientology Offices. It was raining.
 He had walked most of the afternoon. Some secret was taking
 place.

The page was eaten for money.

He didn't know that she had given the yellow book to at least
 one other person. In this case the number 2 is an enigma.

Defraction. Nails. Planks. Hillsides. We *were* leaves.

This city has five streets which open to no.

My three boys are even more like flags when they throw their
 oatmeal into the air.

November sun: the red car approaches the small beyond small town
 but does not yield at the sign near the park. One sound is
 "never" and another a yellow leap. A horse could not breathe
 until now.

Interviewers: like waves, thousands of whys.

Interviewers: this heavy spring I am pretending to read *Sophie's
 Choice*. I have ADD and don't know it. My friend Don has AIDS
 and doesn't know it.

Interviewers: past lives, the sea in front of the house belongs to
 whom? I know in back of the house it belongs to the property
 of the W's, but in front of the house it belongs to…

Page: it was raining on us until they opened a forest in the library.

A sail and a card with a picture of a sail. A son's face, a first
    son, who is now in that phase where his face looks just like
    his mother. A name, a blackboard. Buy this blackboard, because
    the riddled small white marks over all this time make it look
    in its damage like a possible mathematical model for the cosmos.
    Who knows?, the tone of this blackboard might be just what the
    cosmos needs.
The truth is I love you. Above all else, above all trains.
One of the bowls lands on Avenue Yes.
It is three o'clock. One is an X. One is a name.

Thinly Disguised Persons

Places between the letters in words. You know them as well as I know them.

I know you took the book. I know you will not give the book back. In this case it doesn't matter because I borrowed K's copy of K's book.

About five times a year my very first thought upon waking is When did I last see my copy of _____ by _____. This morning it was Vallejo. Where is Vallejo's *Trilce*.

The emphasis of *mine* is a weight.

My first guess is that M took Vallejo… A small bird alights from different branch to different branch among the branches of the small bush. The bird is paradise.

Anyone I suspect of taking any book over the past decade I will refer to as M. There is no M, but in this way I can talk freely. Why would I not want to use an appropriate initial which would hint or aim at the person(s) I suspect. Is an initial a letter? Am I afraid of the person(s) or am I afraid of the initial (letter). Am I afraid of Vallejo.

Another M did not steal anything, nor is this another M suspected of anything. But this M has (unless discarded or given away in the past decade) my original second-hand copy of *Brazilian Poetry*. I would like this back. Today a few minutes ago I opened a package from a book distributor I had been waiting to open. It is another printing of *Brazilian Poetry*. I want to send M this copy asking for my original second-hand copy in return, in return for… as Vallejo is translated by Hays in "Distant Footsteps" "…it will be I." Or will it— this is what I fear—it will not be

I who asks for one book in return for another book. It will be someone
else. It will not be the person I am. The person I am wants to write
to this another M about many things but is afraid to say so. The person
I am wants many other books I left behind in return for something I would
now send.

Clothing is wanted too.

Being shot at.

Lovers and other friends.

Clocks on a purse — woman you dream of turns up next to you on second
day. Secret day. No shoes.

When elephants weep.

A butterfly (yellow/black/brown/white) is draining nectar from white
flowers. A few inches away now a yellow-jacket (black/yellow) is at
work too. At play. At being.

The namingly ends. A lifeless life.
"I would like these if the houses weren't red."

Givingly.
"I have new glasses."

"I can't think without memory."
"Things become is."

The second M also has Duchamp.
The shadow of the telephone pole upon the street is intersected
by other shadows.

Told Some Realisms and Truisms

It isn't time for the house to fall
but it falls anyway. the man drinks
too much and drives through the garage
and onto the porch, the woman gives
notice and walks slowly now toward a
lone tree near the Americana Baseball
Field at the block's end. At day's
end she is sitting there, herself and
as a friend once said while reading
Isaac Babel under lamplight upon another
porch in another American city "beside
herself." Wondering about being beside
herself, being, being short, and still
another woman who said "I was told some
realisms and truisms and I am going to
tell you some. But first I will listen
and let you talk." She starts to talk
now, after all these dreamed endings,
and will drive she decides to the city
where old friends still read Isaac Babel
stories in less than the best light,
where subjects strike your life too quickly,
but from stories more often than a fist
or car in life. Isaac Babel's glasses,
somewhere in his disappearance and murder.
Isaac Babel's glasses making realisms
and truisms into another and others' lives.

— in memory of Richard

Unimportant Shadow

I thought I knew you but I know thought,
my sense of myself and you today is illusion
or delusion, or something unimportant among
the houses and the streets and the trees
and the children and the black glass of the
sea—

words are not seas, not black glass

words are seas, are black glass

one is singular in delusion

one is twice in illusion until the sea comes

the sea comes the sea

—I thought I knew you but it was as if
    I knew thought, thought knew you

—Celan's clinkergame
    Jean's shadow book

—your house up against the unimportant shadow

—your bright black glass north, south

—my sense of myself as childhood
  staying snow

—don't dismiss anything or anyone by saying
  by saying unimportant so

Unseen Information

Maybe I would call it Unseen Information just to give it a name.
When we are making love intensely, very intensely, I always have
the same feeling, that we are so to speak from somewhere else. That
we knew each other in some deep cellular way many years ago, except that
years fades as the appropriate word or term to use. There is some other
feel to the "time." Visual, imagistic.

—smells even, not us but of different seasons, locales, as if some
kind of past had a smell

—and sometimes there is tin to the sound or leaves to the sound or green
to the sound

—and sometimes glass is in the sound, not broken but hanging, or like
a window opening to some sky or tree I had no way of knowing quite like
that before

—and this unspeakable feeling that there is information we are bringing
to each other and cells and fibers of our lives from some place we have
each become a metaphor for, or I assume I have because you have, but (and
I want to say of course) but of course I don't feel you necessarily per-
ceiving me that way, but in some completely silent way I sense it must
but taking place

—and what is sometimes frightening is the metaphor, or the mask—because
because we are not together it always or almost always takes us literal
time (one day, tow days, three days) to agonizingly reach this field,
because of course

the world has taken over, and to take ourselves into such a deep slightly
other place leaves some other sense of the world behind, or aside, and

one of the fears is that we will simply have to part soon again, after
this other is again in our breathing living experience, and to part so
soon after this place makes me think (now thinking returns more fully)
that I will be abandoned by this metaphor, or this mask is only a mask,

or this metaphor is doing something *to* me, like a visitation I cannot
understand—

so this is why we always have to hesitate to be there or almost always,
not because of what is there, because that is dwelling, but in the fear
of having to be back in the world literally without it or us or a cause
or a chance at it again

—sometimes I feel we just need to live and we will know

—there is nothing to do in this silence, it will inform us in unseen ways

it already has

it seems as if we have both felt that

—emptiness almost seems eager at me the afternoon of your departure

—I want to become anything or one you want me to become

—want to become anyone you want me to become

— name thaw, when we say each other in the near past
— name thaw

name thaw in the accidental face you saw

name thaw in forgiveness

name thaw in the last child which fevered your body — some child of poverty
and war—whose child is this name thaw

Vanishing Point

she asked me my name and my address and my phone number
and when she asked me my vocation and i said i was a writer

she asked me if 'writer' had two 't'-s or one. i told her one.
usually it is my name people ask me how to spell—they want to

insert an 'h' or some other extra letter or they don't hear the 'k' as a 'k'
but as an 'a' or as a vanishing point since 'a' follows the 'k.'

the other day on the other phone with another receptionist
i knew she was not hearing me too well and when we reviewed my last name

a second time i gave her the first three letters and then said 'k'
and then said "as in 'kafka.'" it felt very good to say this

and it also make it very clear it was a 'k.'
i wondered only for a moment or two later if the woman on the other end

had 1) heard of kafka 2) liked kafka — and now it occurs to me
that if i do this 'k' as in 'kafka' enough

sooner or later 1) there is bound to be a question 2) something may start up
where kafka becomes a word for something else, some other condition,

some other fact.

write down in your notebook

write down in your notebook
the day you sought jobs "teaching
English as a second language."
You figured since you did not know
any moment of any of these languages
mentioned you could be perfect—you
would never be able to say or write
anything down except in the language
"they" were supposed to learn. Yes,
it was "them" you wanted to teach
in a real ungenerous way I guess. I
had access to a dark blue typewriter
which made typing all these last-minute-
applications easy on the eyes, but the
lousy coffee in mucho amounts overcame
that plus. And the cigarettes, and then
the booze, and showing up to write the
last of the few letters now at midnight
only to find the writer-friend you're
modeling this on was there finishing up
his applications: time to show him your
letters are duplicating his, you jerk.
He doesn't really care and he means it.
He's a fatalist of sorts. This is a
second-person-world and a third-person-
world you've been in for a couple of years
now. Write down in your notebook Where

the hell is I, I who would be seen as selfish
and too much self, but really where is I?
Write down in your notebook supposed
location of this I.

Your Door's Words

You enter and
a ghost eats
your door's words.
Perfect endings

to perfect babies.
Loved you in Florida,
loved by you
on Jane's floor.

We were both
visiting, but we
could not get
lost. Taxis

liked the rain.
The cemetery looked
as expensive
as a mob.

You penetrated me.
Years. Hills.

Author Notes

"Thank You" is based upon Kenneth Koch's *Rose, Where Did You Get That Red?* (Teaching Great Poetry to Children), 1990, (Vintage Books). All the poetry quotes in "Thank You" are, as indicated in the poem, by various children Koch had taught at various sites.

"I have a yellow heart" is from Pablo Neruda's poem "Otro" ("Another"), from William O'Daly's translation of Neruda's book *El corazón amarillo* (The Yellow Heart)

About the Author

Michael Burkard is the author of numerous books of poetry, including most recently *Envelope of Night: Selected and Uncollected Poems 1966-1990* (Nightboat, 2008), and several books of drawings. He teaches at Syracuse University.

Acknowledgements

The poems in this book were first published in the following magazines: *American Poetry Review, Bat City Review, Black Clock, Caketrain, Conduit, Denver Quarterly, 88, Fence, Gulf Coast, jubilat, Lit, The Louisville Review, lyric, The Onset Review, Smartish Pace, 3rd Bed, Verbal Seduction* and *Verse.*

"a cloud of dusk" appeared in *The Best American Poetry, 2004*, edited by David Lehman and Lyn Hejinian (Scribner Poetry); "Black Horses in White Envelopes" appeared in *A Best of Fence, Vol. 1*, edited by Rebecca Wolff (Fence Books), and "can't meet the wind" appeared in *Shade, an anthology, 2004*, edited by David Dodd Lee (Four Way Books).

ISBN: 978-0-9844598-1-0

Design and typesetting by HR Hegnauer
Cover drawing by Michael Burkard
Text set in Garamond & American Typewriter

Cataloging-in-publication data is available
From the Library of Congress

Distributed by University Press of New England
One Court Street
Lebanon, NH 03766
www.upne.com

Nightboat Books
Callicoon, New York
www.nightboat.org

Nightboat Books

Nightboat Books, a nonprofit organization, seeks to develop audiences for writers whose work resists convention and transcends boundaries. We publish books rich with poignancy, intelligence, and risk. Please visit our website, www.nightboat.org, to learn about our titles and how you can support our future publications.

The following individuals have supported the publication of this book. We thank them for their generosity and commitment to the mission of Nightboat Books:

Kazim Ali
Jennifer Chapis
Sarah Heller
Elizabeth Motika
Laura Sejen
Benjamin Taylor

This book has been made possible, in part, by a grant from the New York State Council on the Arts Literature Program.

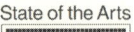
State of the Arts

NYSCA